BMW EfficientDynamics
Less emissions. More driving pleasure.

The new BMW Z4.
Evidence that engineering is an art form.

The new BMW Z4

www.bmw.co.uk
Tel. 0800 777 137

The Ultimate Driving Machine

10.4 – 46.3 mpg (7.0 – 6.1 ltr/100km). Combined 30.1 – 34.4 mpg (9.4 – 8.2 ltr/100km). CO_2 emissions 219 – 192 g/km.

Contents: Issue 16, Summer 2009

The Futurists' notoriously antagonistic performances were rooted in provocation, subversion and scandal and formed the precedent for an art form embracing audience interaction and participation. They commenced a genealogy of participatory art which runs through Dada, Situationism and Allan Kaprow's happenings. And, as Claire Bishop and Boris Groys illustrate, their influence on contemporary practice continues. — *Plus:* Adrien Sina and Sarah Wilson celebrate the work of Valentine Saint-Point, the unsung heroine of Futurism.

Gigantic construction sites, mining pits, hydroelectric dams, polar regions, Soviet cosmodromes and Chinese cities… Armin Linke scrutinises such places with a visual awareness that draws them back from the realms of unfamiliarity into a frame that surrenders the vast scenes depicted to reactions of reverie and contemplation. Kurt Forster discusses Linke's recent documentation of the Alps and the influence of Italian painter Giovanni Segantini in their common gravitation towards the sublime.

To coincide with Tate Britain's Richard Long retrospective, Robert Macfarlane looks at the importance of walking in his work, and reminds us how Long differs from those "American romantic roadsters" (Thoreau, Emerson, John Muir) in that he is "far less interested in reflection than in motion, and less in mind than in body". Long's art is also inextricably linked to his childhood. As he himself has said: "Why stop skimming stones when you grow up?" — *Plus:* Carl Andre pens an appreciation to his old friend.

Tate Liverpool's 'Colour Chart' exhibition looks at the moment in the twentieth century when a group of artists began to perceive colour as a readymade rather than in purely scientific or expressive terms. The gallery's director talks to one of its leading practitioners, while David Batchelor muses on his motives for making monochromes. — *Plus:* François Morellet talks about the making of his painting *Random Distribution of 40,000 Squares using the odd and Even Numbers of a Telephone Directory.*

Last year one of the largest donations of art in Britain was made by Anthony d'Offay. The collection of more than 700 works by leading artists, known as ARTIST ROOMS and assembled over the past 28 years, is now owned jointly by the National Galleries of Scotland and Tate on behalf of the nation. This year Tate sites, the National Galleries of Scotland and thirteen museums and galleries across the UK are showing more than 30 ARTIST ROOMS in what is the first tour of the collection. TATE ETC. talks to Anthony d'Offay about the impetus behind the project, and also to a selection of the artists on display.

THOMAS JOSHUA COOPER
TRUE

·

1st — 30th May 2009

Thomas Joshua Cooper
Blinding brightness, Yankee Harbour.
Greenwich Island. The South Shetland Islands,
United Kingdom, Antarctica. 62° 32' S., 2008
Gelatin Silver Print, 71×91cm

HAUNCH OF VENISON LONDON

6 Burlington Gardens
London W1S 3ET
United Kingdom

T +44 (0) 20 7495 5050
F +44 (0) 20 7495 4050
london@haunchofvenison.com
www.haunchofvenison.com

For the latest Duveen Commission at Tate Britain, Eva Rothschild has created a startling new sculpture that will weave its way through the gallery's central space, reflecting her previous work's blending of contemporary interpretations of sculptural traditions with her distinctive voice.

To coincide with Tate Modern's exhibition of paintings by the Danish artist, Robert Storr examines the career of Per Kirkeby – from his Pop motifs borrowed from Hergé's Tintin books to his monumental architectonic sculptures.

How do we come to remember an artwork? So often paintings remain, by and large, immemorial, existing as fragmentary shards of recollection, their compositions pieced together from the allusions and associations embedded in the first encounter. Geoff Dyer reflects on this shaky process of memorisation in his return to Turner's *Figures in a Building*, constructing an image built from analogies as broad as Andrei Tarkovsky's *Stalker* and the exclusion zone surrounding the abandoned Chernobyl nuclear power station.

John Cage famously said that musicians in the post-war world had to learn from visual artists, while Frank O'Hara called himself a "sweeper-up after artists". Collaboration, interaction or simple conversations between artists and poets have a fruitful history – from Blaise Cendrars and artist Sonia Delaunay to Barry Schwabsky and Katharina Grosse. What is it, Vincent Katz asks, that fascinates artists about those in other fields, drawing them across the lines to work together?

As a year-long season of exhibitions focusing on Polish art begins across the country, TATE ETC. brings together four Polish art professionals to discuss the reasons why the visual arts produced after 1945 in Poland are not better known abroad.

A look at John William Inchbold's *Suggestive Study, Paradise (Head of a Girl and a Bird of Paradise)* through the lens of Darwinian biology; a first-person perspective of a muse within the seventeenth-century painting *The Cholmondeley Ladies*; reflections on a past meeting between Carol Bove and Daria Martin evoke a reappraisal of the term "body weather"; and artist-turned-chef Valentine Warner, inspired by Charles Collins's painting *Lobster on a Delft Dish*, writes a lobster recipe especially for TATE ETC.

On his first visit to the Tate archive, Travis Elborough finds his mind going pleasurably adrift over a photograph of two unidentified men by the seaside found amid Francis Bacon's archives.

Editors' Note

In 1913 the Futurist F T Marinetti printed the *Variety Theatre Manifesto*, which was designed to provoke and scandalise its audience. Suggestions included "spreading powerful glue on some of the seats" and offering free tickets to people who were "notoriously unbalanced, irritable or eccentric". Of course, Marinetti and company thought they were being hilarious, but they also had serious intentions. As Boris Groys points out in his conversation with Claire Bishop[page 30], they wished to "destroy the long-held benign contemplative attitude of the spectator, which had been the standard position of art audiences in the nineteenth century". To this they added their unsavoury alliance with fascist ideology to create what was arguably the most vibrant and disruptive art movement of the twentieth century. It was destined to fail. However, their attitude would shape generations of future artists, activists and thinkers – from Tristan Tzara to Guy Debord, Allan Kaprow to Maurizio Cattelan. Now, it is fair to say that participation and collaboration have become the mainstays of contemporary art methodology, perhaps nowhere better exemplified than in Polish artist Artur Zmijewski's film *Them* (2007).[page 40 and page 96] This engrossing piece focuses on a series of painting workshops between four different ideological groups: Jews, the socialists, Polish nationalists and the Catholic church. Each is asked to make an image that represents their identity, and the results are discussed collectively. Inevitably, polite comment descends into chaos and bitter exchanges. Despite Zmijewski's cool, subjective editing, the complexity of a nation's image of itself is brought alive in fifteen minutes. No doubt Marinetti would have approved.

Bice Curiger & Simon Grant

–We need good, smart and direct Art, as long as it doesn't hurt!

Samuel Nyholm
Untitled (Good, Smart and Direct Art) (2009)
Ink on paper
30 × 50 cm

TATEETC.

Editorial Director – *Bice Curiger*
Editor – *Simon Grant*
Editorial Assistant – *Mariko Finch*
Art Director – *Cornel Windlin*
Designer – *Alex Rich*
Production Editor – *Ian Massey*
Interns – *Nils Svensk, Aaron Juneau, Justyna Sowa*
Acting Publisher – *Phil Allison*
Associate Publisher –
    Naomi Richmond-Swift
Director, Tate Media – *Will Gompertz*

Special thanks –
Hannah Barry at Anthony d'Offay, Sadie Coles, Emily Palmer, Sarah Haviland and Nicola Vanstone at Cultureshock Media, Mary Dean, Ellsworth Kelly, François, Danielle and Frederic Morellet, Anna Mroczkowska, Mini and Seymour Rich, Aneta Prasal-Wisniewska, Simon Prosser, Karol Sienkiewicz, Simon Wilson

Erratum –
In issue 15, Martin Herbert's piece on page 65 omitted to include a caption for Denise Kum's piece Flotilla, *for which we apologise*

TATE ETC.
Millbank
London SW1P 4RG
Phone +44 20 7887 8724
Fax +44 20 7887 3940
www.tate.org.uk/tateetc

Editorial — +44 20 7887 8724
tateetc@tate.org.uk
Tate Membership enquiries —
+ 44 20 7887 8888
membership@tate.org.uk
Subscriptions — +44 20 7887 8959
subscriptions@tate.org.uk
Advertising — Cultureshock Media Ltd,
27b Tradescant Road, London SW8 1XD
+44 20 7735 9263
ads@cultureshockmedia.co.uk

Distributed internationally and in the UK by COMAG Specialist +44 1895 433 800
Central Books +44 845 458 9925

Printing — St Ives (Plymouth) Ltd
Reprographics — DawkinsColour, London

Bonhams
1793

20th Century British Art
Wednesday 1 July
New Bond Street
Entries now invited

Works by leading British Artists of the
20th Century remain highly sought after at
auction and there is a lot of demand for works
by elite figures of the period such as Robert
Bevan, David Bomberg, Dame Elisabeth Frink,
Dame Barbara Hepworth, Patrick Heron, Ivon
Hitchens, Augustus John, L S Lowry, Sir William
Nicholson, Ben Nicholson, Eric Ravilious, Graham
Sutherland, William Turnbull and Keith Vaughan
among many others.

The sale closes for consignments on Monday
18 May.

To discuss your collecting needs or to obtain
a free and confidential sale valuation, without
obligation, please contact one of our Specialists.

Matthew Bradbury
+44 (0) 20 7468 8295
Lizzie Hill
+44 (0) 20 7468 8365
Penny Day
+44 (0) 20 7468 8366
Chris Dawson
+44 (0) 20 7468 8296

email: britart@bonhams.com

Catalogue
+44 (0) 1666 502 200
subscriptons@bonhams.com

Illustrated:
Sir Stanley Spencer R.A. (1891-1959)
Primroses
oil on canvas
Estimate: £20,000 - 25,000
To be included in the 1 July sale

Bonhams
101 New Bond Street, London W1S 1SR
www.bonhams.com/20cbritish

London · New York · Paris · San Francisco · Los Angeles · Hong Kong · Melbourne · Dubai   www.bonhams.com

Beuys Is Here

An exhibition of sculptures, drawings, posters and multiples by Joseph Beuys
4 July – 27 September

de la warr pavilion
www.dlwp.com

ARTIST ROOMS

ON TOUR WITH

The Art Fund

TATE    NATIONAL GALLERIES OF SCOTLAND

SHOW RCA 2009

FOUR EXHIBITIONS OF CONTEMPORARY WORK BY NEW ARTISTS AND DESIGNERS

SHOW SCULPTURE
28 May – 7 June
15–25 Howie Street,
London SW11 4AS

SHOW ONE
29 May – 7 June
Fine Art, Applied Art

SHOW FASHION
10 June, 4pm & 7pm
Tickets must be purchased
in advance by calling
020 7590 4566 or visiting
www.rca.ac.uk

SHOW TWO
26 June – 5 July
(closed 3 July)
Architecture & Design,
Communications, Design
for Production, Fashion &
Textiles, Humanities

All SHOW RCA exhibitions
(except SHOW SCULPTURE)
take place at:
Royal College of Art
Kensington Gore
London SW7 2EU

For more information
and opening times please
visit www.rca.ac.uk or
call the SHOW RCA hotline
on 020 7590 4498

Free admission
(except SHOW FASHION)

Royal College of Art
Postgraduate Art and Design

CONRAN FOUNDATION
DESIGN FOR QUALITY OF LIFE

Interbrand

launching the Kettle's Yard Development Appeal

Kettle's Yard at Tate Britain

9 May - 14 June 2009
Tate Britain gallery 23

KETTLE'S YARD at TATE BRITAIN:
including Gaudier-Brzeska,
Brancusi, Miró, Nicholson
and specially commissioned works by
Edmund de Waal and Gary Woodley

KETTLE'S YARD

KETTLE'S YARD in CAMBRIDGE:
exhibition: Material Intelligence
16 May - 12 July 2009
Castle Street, Cambridge CB3 0AQ
t 01223 748100 • www.kettlesyard.co.uk

gallery: Tuesday-Sunday 11.30am-5pm
house: Tuesdays-Sundays 1.30-4.30pm
admission free

Three Projects: Venice 2009

Turning Point South East:
Developing Contemporary Visual Art in South East England

Milton Keynes Gallery

James Lee Byars Lived Here
4 June – 5 July 2009

Palazzo Pesaro Papafava
Calle de la Rachetta
Cannaregio 3764
80121 Venice
Open daily 12.00–18.00

www.mk-g.org

Image courtesy Michael Werner Gallery, Berlin, Cologne and New York. © Estate of James Lee Byars

de la warr pavilion

**Ulrike and Eamon Compliant:
An interactive project by Blast Theory**
4–7 June 2009

Palazzo Zenobio
Fondamenta del Soccorso
Dorsoduro 2596, Venice
Open: Tuesday – Sunday 10.00–18.00

www.dlwp.com

ArtSway
Contemporary Visual Art in the New Forest

ArtSway's New Forest Pavilion
Previews: 4–6 June 2009
Open: 7–28 June 2009

Jordan Baseman, Alex Frost, Dinu Li,
Hannah Maybank, Nathaniel Mellors

Palazzo Zenobio
Fondamenta del Soccorso
Dorsoduro 2596, Venice
Open: Tuesday – Sunday 10.00–18.00

www.artsway.org.uk

53. Esposizione
Internazionale
d'Arte
Eventi collaterali
la Biennale di Venezia

the **arts institute** at bournemouth

Hampshire
County Council

Hallett Independent
ART INSURANCE WITH A DIFFERENCE

Supported by
**ARTS COUNCIL
ENGLAND**

Turning Point South East
Developing Contemporary Visual Art in South East England

**BRITISH
COUNCIL**

LOTTERY FUNDED

TAKE YOUR TIME OLAFUR ELIASSON
MAY 1 – SEPTEMBER 13

The
Photographers'
Gallery

**Also showing
Dark is the Night:
Jordan Baseman**

Catherine Yass, *Damage/burn/canal,* 2005. Courtesy the artist and Alison Jacques Gallery, London.

The Photographic Object
24 April –14 June 2009

Admission Free
16 –18 Ramillies St.
London W1F 7LW
⊖ Oxford Circus
www.photonet.org.uk

The Photographers' Gallery is a
registered charity no. 262548.

ARTS COUNCIL ENGLAND

SCHAULAGER ®

HOLBEIN
TO
TILLMANS

Metròpolis

Tensió el segon dia de vaga del taxi

12 GEN

PROMINENT GUESTS FROM THE KUNSTMUSEUM BASEL

04.04. – 04.10.2009

Tue, Wed, Fri, noon–6 p.m.; Thu, noon–7 p.m.; Sat, Sun, 10 a.m.–5 p.m./Open on Labour Day, Ascension Day, Whitsunday and 1 August.
During Art Basel: 8–9 and 11–14 June, 10 a.m.–6 p.m.; 10 June, noon–6 p.m.

Schaulager, Ruchfeldstrasse 19, CH-4142 Münchenstein/Basel, www.schaulager.org

LAURENZ FOUNDATION

BILL VIOLA

ARTIST ROOMS

ON TOUR WITH

June 19 - September 5 2009
The Pier Arts Centre
Stromness Orkney
www.pierartscentre.com

Supported by

The Scottish
Government
Riaghaltas na h-Alba

Catherine's Room, 2001   photo Kira Perov

Presented in collaboration with Bill Viola Studio and with the support of Haunch of Venison

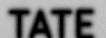

NATIONAL
GALLERIES OF
SCOTLAND

pier
arts centre

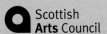
Scottish
Arts Council

ORKNEY
ISLANDS COUNCIL

ef Esmée
Fairbairn
FOUNDATION

The Pier Arts Centre
is a Registered Scottish
Charity No SC014815

Barry Flanagan
Hare Coursed

NewArtCentre.

Roche Court
East Winterslow
Salisbury, Wiltshire
SP5 1BG

T +44 (0) 1980 862244
F +44 (0) 1980 862447
nac@sculpture.uk.com
www.sculpture.uk.com

Barry Flanagan
Hare Coursed
16 May - 6 September 2009

NewArtCentre.

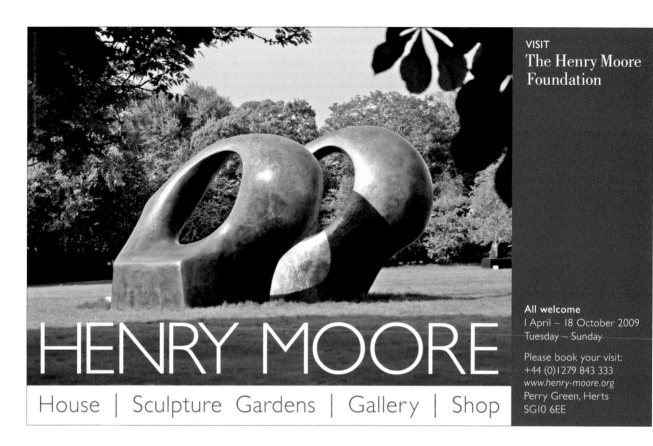

ROYAL OPERA HOUSE

BOOK NOW
SUMMER SEASON

For cast details and to book online visit
www.roh.org.uk

Box Office
020 7304 4000
(Mon-Sat 10am-8pm)

Opera and Music

NEW PRODUCTION
LULU
Alban Berg
4 - 20 June
£4 - £100

UN BALLO IN MASCHERA
Giuseppe Verdi
26 June - 17 July
£7 - £125
Generously supported by
The Friends of Covent Garden

LA TRAVIATA
Giuseppe Verdi
18 June - 6 July
£9 - £210
Production generously sponsored by

Generous philanthropic support
from Peter Borender (Director's Circle) and
Mrs Aline Foriel- Destezet (Ambassador)

LIVE to BP Summer Big Screens on 30 June*

IL BARBIERE DI SIVIGLIA
Gioachino Rossini
4 - 18 July
£8 - £180

LIVE to BP Summer Big Screens on 15 July*

TOSCA
Giacomo Puccini
9 -18 July
£9 - £210

ROLANDO VILLAZÓN & ANTONIO PAPPANO IN CONCERT
24 June at 7.30pm
£4 - £85

JETTE PARKER YOUNG ARTISTS SUMMER CONCERT
19 July at 3pm
£5 - £35
The Jette Parker Young Artists Programme
is generously supported by Oak
Foundation

NEW PRODUCTION
PARTHENOGENESIS
James MacMillan
11 - 18 June
£9.50 - £24
Linbury Studio Theatre

Ballet and Dance

ONDINE
Frederick Ashton
27 May - 6 June
£5 - £85 eves
£4 - £60 mats

LIVE to BP Summer Big Screens on 3 June*

JEWELS
George Balanchine
9 - 19 June
£5 - £85
Production originally sponsored (2007) by

 Van Cleef & Arpels

Generous philanthropic support (2007)
from Dianne and Michael Bienes
('Diamonds').

UK PREMIERE
WUTHERING HEIGHTS
Cathy Marsden / Bern Ballet
27 - 30 May
£7.50 - £19
Linbury Studio Theatre

*For BP Summer Big Screen information go to www.roh.org.uk/bpbigscreens

Main image: Renée Fleming, Soprano, The Royal Opera. Photograph: Jason Bell
Behind the scenes photography: Rob Moore

ROYAL OPERA HOUSE | A WORLD STAGE | WATCH IT COME ALIVE AT www.roh.org.uk

6 CHARACTERS SEARCH OF an author

what for YOU is an iLLusion that You Have to CREATE, for us on the OTHER hand is our sole REALITY

SaRa FaNELLi
29 APRiL - 20 JUNE
TUE - FRi : 12 - 6pm,
SAT : 12 - 4pm,
MON : BY APPOINTMENT
entry free

stanleypickergallery:

Kingston University London
www.stanleypickergallery.org
FACULTY of ART, DESIGN & ARCHITECTURE, KINGSTON UNIVERSITY, KNIGHTS PARK, KINGSTON UPON THAMES KT1 2QJ

Howard Hodgkin

Howard Hodgkin
June – 11 July 2009

The Alan Cristea Gallery at
31&34 Cork St. London W1S 3NU
Telephone +44 (0) 20 7439 1866
Facsimile +44 (0) 20 7439 1874
Email: info@alancristea.com
Website: www.alancristea.com

Sweet Bowl
1967

Ruins
1964

Patrick Caulfield
Prints 1964 –1999
14 July – 5 September 2009

The **Alan Cristea Gallery** at
31&34 Cork St. London W1S 3NU
Telephone +44 (0)20 7439 1866
Facsimile +44 (0)20 7439 1874
Email: info@alancristea.com
Website: www.alancristea.com

OLIVER BARRATT
BETWEEN THE LINES
7 MAY — 6 JUNE 2009

BEARDSMORE
GALLERY

22—— Prince of Wales Road
London NW5 3LG
+44 (0)20 7485 092
info@beardsmoregallery.com
www.beardsmoregallery.com

Design: www.graphicswithart.com

MICHAEL TYZACK

(1933-2007)

28TH MAY - 12TH JUNE 2009

catalogue available

PORTLAND GALLERY

8 BENNET STREET · LONDON SW1A 1RP
TELEPHONE 020 7493 1888 · FAX 020 7499 4353 · EMAIL art@portlandgallery.com

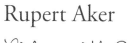

Rupert Aker

'Cider with Rosie'

Celebrating 50 years since the publication of
Laurie Lee's classic autobiography: 1959-2009
Paintings of the cotswold Slad valley as it is today.

Chelsea Gallery, The Reference Library,
Chelsea Old Town Hall, King's Road, London SW3 5EZ
5-9 May 2009
Tues 14.00-20.00
Wednesday, Friday and Saturday 09.30-17.00
Thursday 09.30-20.00

Also at:
Town Hall, Victoria Square,
Painswick, Gloucestershire GL6 6QA
6-7 June 2009 10.30-17.00

Gardens Gallery, Montpellier Gardens,
Cheltenham, Gloucestershire GL50 1UW
12-18 August 2009 10.00-17.30

*Never to be forgotten, that first long drink of golden
fire, juice of those valleys and of that time, wine of wild
orchards, of russet summer, of plump red apples and
Rosie's burning cheeks. Never to be forgotten, or ever
tasted again'* Laurie Lee, Cider with Rosie

For more information visit www.rupertaker.co.uk
and www.myspace.com/rupertaker

Diarmuid Kelley

Autumn Journal

15 May - 2 June 2009

Offer Waterman & Co
11 Langton Street
London SW10 0JL
+44 (0)20 7351 0068
info@waterman.co.uk

An illustrated catalogue accompanies the exhibition.
For more details, please contact the gallery or view online.

www.waterman.co.uk

Susan Collins
Seascape

4 April – 15 June

Seascape Bexhill, 29 October 2008 16:55

An exhibition combining digital technologies with the classical traditions of English landscape painting
www.dlwp.com

This image is available as a signed print exclusively from the De La Warr Pavilion for the duration of the exhibition.
£55 unframed, call 01424 229 111 for details.
www.dlwp.com/susancollins

de la warr pavilion

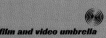

film and video umbrella

Arts & Humanities Research Council

ARTS COUNCIL ENGLAND

CLIFFORD ROSS
PHOTOGRAPHY: BEYOND REALISM
28 April – 19 June 2009

Mountain IV, 2005, 190 x 330 cm

ROBILANT + VOENA
1st Floor & 2nd Floor, 38 Dover Street, London W1S 4NL, UK
T. +44 (0)20 7409 1540, edmondo@dirobilant.com
www.robilantvoena.com

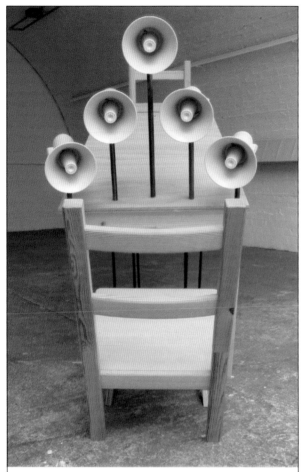

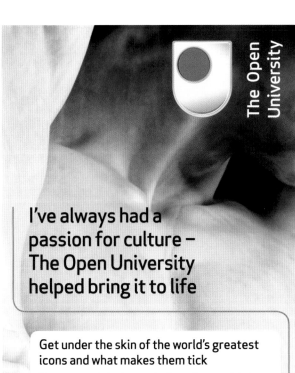

GOING AND RETURNING
(Itus et Reditus)

Jonathan Adamson   Pam Day   Andrew Darke
www.p-l-a-c-e.org

"...It is, on the whole, my best church..."
Sir George Gilbert Scott - All Souls' Church, Halifax

Pam Day Ladder, Plates and Sheet, 2007   St. Stephen's Church, Halifax

ALL SOULS' CHURCH, Haley Hill, Halifax, HX3 6DR. **9-14 June 2009 and Saturdays until 18 July, inclusive.** And BANKFIELD MUSEUM (adjacent, in Akroyd Park), Boothtown Road, Halifax, HX3 6HG, tel. 01422 352334. **9 June - 18 July 2009, inclusive.** Opening times: Tuesday - Saturday 10am - 5pm and Sundays 1 - 4pm. Closed Mondays at both sites.

Calderdale
Council
Libraries, Museums & Arts

THE CHURCHES CONSERVATION TRUST

the new 'clusters' series by Rachel Coad

pack
Australians in London
May 26 – June 6, 2009

Gallery 27

27 Cork Street
Mayfair, London

phone: **+44 (0)20 7734 7595** (during the exhibition)

email: **rachelc@aapt.net.au**
web: **www.rachelcoad.com.au**

Simon Gudgeon
ISIS

To be unveiled in Hyde Park, London this summer
Exhibition opens at 24 Bruton Street, June 2009

HALCYON GALLERY

London Galleries: 24 Bruton Street   29 New Bond Street
24 Bruton Street W1J 6QQ   +44 (0)20 7659 7640   info@halcyongallery.com   www.halcyongallery.com

<u>Futurism & The Art of Participation</u>: As well as being noted for their avant-garde painting, the Futurists' performances were legendary for their intent to provoke and scandalise the public. Often encouraging audience interaction, they led the way for participatory art, from Dada, Situationism and Allan Kaprow's happenings to the present. To coincide with Tate Modern's 'Futurism' exhibition, TATE ETC. brings together two art professionals to explore this history

BRING THE NOISE

BY CLAIRE BISHOP & BORIS GROYS

Costumes by **Fortunato Depero** for his ballet *Machine of 3000* (1924)

Courtesy the Depero Museum, Rovereto

Gerado Dottori
*A Futurist Serata
in Perugia* (1914)
Ink on paper
21×28.5cm

CLAIRE BISHOP   When we talk about participatory art today we often think of it as consensual
and collaborative, but when you look back to the Futurist artists their notion of
participation was designed to provoke, scandalise and agitate the public. You
get a good sense of this in the printed material of the time, such as the *Variety
Theatre Manifesto* of 1913. It included suggestions for disrupting the audience
such as "spreading a powerful glue on some of the seats so that male or female
spectators will stay glued down and make everyone laugh"; "selling the same
ticket to ten people, traffic jam, bickering and wrangling"; "offering free tickets
to gentlemen or ladies who are notoriously unbalanced, irritable or eccentric and
likely to provoke uproars with obscene gestures, pinching women or other
freakishness"; and "sprinkling the seats with dust to make people itch and sneeze".
Are these infantile provocations, or were they aligned with Futurism's political
agenda?

Filippo Tommaso
Marinetti in Paris
in the 1920s

David Burliuk
posing for a
photograph in
New York
(c.1920)

BORIS GROYS

If you read the descriptions of the events that the Futurists organised, you
notice that they always tried to antagonise with gestures, actions and speeches.
One of their most famous declarations was "War, the World's only Hygiene".
Such behaviour provoked anger and even disgust in the public, and aimed
to destroy the long-held benign contemplative attitude of the spectator which
had been the standard position of art audiences in the nineteenth century.
The goal was to involve the audience in an event that was organised and ultimately
controlled by the artist – even if this involvement took an adversarial form.
Better to antagonise the audience than let it remain neutral.

CLAIRE BISHOP

I think it's important that they're using performance as a way to do that, and
specifically using variety theatre as a model for the *serate* (the evening performances).
First, the *serate* were characterised by non-sequential episodes of different types
of performance, such as variety theatre or cabaret (theatrical events, poetry readings,
manifesto readings, etc); secondly, variety theatre is a lower-class mode of
entertainment, and has a greater degree of interaction than conventional bourgeois
theatre. To quote Marinetti in the *Variety Theatre Manifesto* again: "The variety
theatre is alone in seeking the audience's collaboration. It doesn't remain static
like a stupid voyeur but joins noisily in the action, in the singing accompanying
the orchestra, communicating with the actors in surprising actions and bizarre
dialogues." Elsewhere, he talks about people smoking in the auditorium, as it creates
a unifying ambience between the stage and the audience.

BORIS GROYS

At the beginning of the twentieth century people still maintained the tradition of a romantic understanding of art that was characteristic of the nineteenth century. The goal of art was to provoke deep emotions in the soul of the spectator – such as love and admiration. The viewer was supposed to be overwhelmed, especially if it was true, authentic art. However, at the end of the nineteenth century it became quite clear that people remained mostly completely neutral and unaffected by art. This was especially true of the new democratic audiences that were not trained to love it. So the Futurists tried to provoke again deep feelings in the audience – but feelings of hatred, resentment and disgust, rather than admiration and love. However, the goal remained the same romantic goal: to disturb the peace of the audience's mind, to let it be overwhelmed by powerful emotions, albeit negative ones.

CLAIRE BISHOP

Marinetti is quite clear that mass audiences are not to be found through books, and he writes that 90 per cent of the Italian public go to the theatre. So there's a deliberate choice of live performance as a mode of reaching people, which is then backed up by a media campaign, with press releases and reviews being sent out almost immediately after the event.

BORIS GROYS

And it is important to remember that the Futurists often presented themselves as clowns. They painted themselves in different colours, shouted unintelligible words, created "noise music". In their own way, they were reviving the medieval tradition of *Commedia dell'Arte*. The Russian Futurists did the same, using the Russian medieval folkloristic tradition of *lubok* – a kind of comic strip. They also painted their faces, put big wooden spoons in their pockets instead of handkerchiefs and walked through the streets, frightening passers-by.

CLAIRE BISHOP

But did the Russian Futurists back this up with media attention as well?

BORIS GROYS

Absolutely. David Burliuk was especially good at that. He briefed the press before the events took place and organised the scandals. If the scandals didn't take place, he created the illusion of them for the journalists.

CLAIRE BISHOP

But they were not allied to a political position in the way that the Italian Futurists were allied to an agenda of nationalism.

BORIS GROYS

Not at all. I wouldn't say that Russian Futurism was completely free of nationalism, because it was informed and influenced by icon painting, primitive painting, folkloristic poetry and a celebration of Russian provincialism. The Futurists wanted to reveal very deep archaic, even archaeological, layers in the national culture. But they were neither militaristic nor state-orientated. Rather, there was a certain political affiliation between Russian Futurism and Russian anarchism. And the tradition of political anarchism was very strong in Russia.

CLAIRE BISHOP

One could talk about two phases of Italian Futurism: an early one up to about 1917, and after that when it is more aligned to fascism and the work becomes more mediocre.

BORIS GROYS

That's true to an extent, but already by 1909 you see the first manifestation of all the fascist themes in Marinetti's *Futurist Manifesto*. You have this promise of a new, strong, modernised, industrialised Italy coming on to the European scene. It's absolutely impossible to imagine any Russian Futurist poet or painter at that time praising the state, or wanting it to be mobilised and militarised.

CLAIRE BISHOP

But this is also partly a result of Italian art being dominated by such a strong historical tradition since the Renaissance – and wanting to escape from that tradition.

BORIS GROYS — Yes, there is no question about that. On the other hand, Russian art was as dominated by academicism and naturalism as any art of that time.

CLAIRE BISHOP — The three things that characterise Futurism for me are the politics, the provocation and the use of the media. It is rare to find these in equal measure in subsequent art.

BORIS GROYS — Futurism tried to create a total, even totalitarian, space – a space that one cannot escape. It is like the carnivalistic space that was later described by Mikhail Bakhtin. If you are a part of this, you cannot escape being beaten, being insulted, being pissed on, etc. You are pushed into the active position because there is no way out of it. As a spectator you find yourself having to defend yourself against the artist, and in doing so you become a part of the artwork. I think that was a real innovation – making the neutral, spectatorial position impossible, including the spectator by excluding the possibility of being outside.

CLAIRE BISHOP — That's a very good way of putting it. I'm interested in how Italian Futurist performance then develops into Dada, because you can see the same patterns emerging in what took place at the Dada nightclub Cabaret Voltaire (founded by Hugo Ball), but without a defined political position; indeed, they refuse existing positions by embracing nihilism and meaninglessness. One (late) Dada event is worth mentioning in particular, since it breaks with the tradition of cabaret performance. In April 1921 André Breton, Tristan Tzara and others organised a tour around the church of St Julien le Pauvre in Paris – or rather, around its churchyard, which at the time was used as a rubbish dump. In the flyer for the event they billed this as one of several planned tours that wished "to set right the incompetence of suspicious guides" by leading "excursions and visits" to places that have "no reason to exist". Instead of drawing attention to picturesque sites, or places of historical interest or sentimental value, the aim was to make a nonsense of the social form of the guided tour. Like the Futurists, the Dada group also made good use of advertising and press releases to garner media attention (for example, one event in early 1920 had promised an appearance by Charlie Chaplin). A major difference from Futurism occurs when Breton comes to analyse this event (which he saw as a failure and as inducing collective depression): he no longer felt the need to scandalise the public. This becomes an important moment in the transition from Dada to Surrealism. Breton is now not interested in provocation, but in the construction of a moral position.

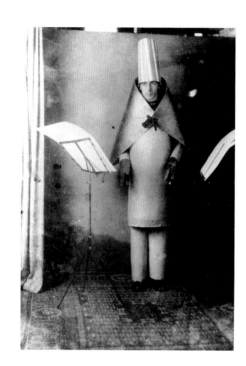

The site of
Hugo Ball's
nightclub
Cabaret
Voltaire as
photographed
in 1935

BORIS GROYS Well, Dadaism was also akin to a certain kind of political anarchism. This is especially clear if one reads Hugo Ball's *Flight out of Time*. After becoming increasingly disillusioned with political anarchism, he also leaves the Dada movement. But in any case there was a difference between Futurism and the Dadaist Cabaret Voltaire or Surrealism. Futurist activities mostly took place in open public spaces. With Cabaret Voltaire you bought tickets and would go willingly to participate, as was the case with those who experienced the tumultuous reaction to Dalí and Buñuel's screening of *Un Chien Andalou*.

CLAIRE BISHOP I can't imagine there being a similar reaction today to a work of art. Maybe these reports of outrage in the face of avant-garde production in the 1920s are idealised. But maybe it is also the case that viewers would attend such events precisely for the pleasure of responding with outrage to provocation.

BORIS GROYS There have been different sensibilities. If you read, for example, the diary entries of people from across the centuries about their experiences in front of art, what is interesting is that some were so impressed by a Raphael or a Leonardo da Vinci painting that they fainted, or would lose their appetite, or couldn't sleep. In descriptions of the events at Cabaret Voltaire, there are many examples of people who fainted or needed medical help. Also in the Russian audience of the same time, some people almost lost consciousness when Mayakovsky allegedly said: "Pushkin should be thrown out from the ship of contemporaneity."

CLAIRE BISHOP Do you think there's a connecting emotion? One is out of shock and the other out of pleasure?

BORIS GROYS For a very long time people believed that there were certain religious, spiritual, moral and aesthetic values that lay at the basis of human civilisation, society, even everyday life. They thought that if these were put in question, attacked and lost, then the very basis of their existence would dissolve, everything would collapse and they just would not survive this general catastrophe. Today, nobody believes that ideal values build the fundament of our civilisation, so one can faint only at the news about a financial crisis. Earlier one believed that one could be killed by art – in a certain magical way. Then art overcomes a distance between the spectator and itself and reaches and penetrates the spectator somehow. At the beginning of the nineteenth century you were supposed to create something so beautiful that the spectator could not escape the spell of this beauty. Or something so terrible, so ugly and repulsive that he or she could not escape the shock. But I won't say that the goal here is different. The goal is to create something that is so powerful that it undermines the capability of neutral, peaceful contemplation.

CLAIRE BISHOP   When looking at participatory art of later decades, such as the happenings, we can see that they are also coercive. For example, in some of Allan Kaprow's happenings the script defined the action and everyone participated together, with no space for critical reflection. This is slightly different from the Situationists' approach to collaborative events; some accounts exist that analyse and examine the *dérive*. The Situationist group, particularly as theorised by Guy Debord in the 1960s, wished to suppress art – but in order to realise it as life. We could see this as another way of eliminating a spectatorial position. It's not about one group who do, and another group who watch or observe, contemplating the products of others. Throughout the 1960s we find different modes of participation taking place in art, all done in the name of various types of emancipation. With happenings in France, produced and theorised by Jean-Jacques Lebel, it is a sexual emancipation of the body; with Kaprow participation is figured more as a kind of existential awakening that would enable participants to have a more perceptive, responsive approach to the world.

BORIS GROYS   Well, everything is always about emancipation. The whole modern European culture is about emancipation. But I think the question is: emancipation from what? If you look at the late 1940s and 1950s, then it is emancipation from totalitarian space. Everything was about existentialism, about finding your true self and so on. Then suddenly in the 1960s one has a wave of a reprocessing of the totalitarian past and domestication of the totalitarian experience inside a stable framework of liberal democracies. Then it is understood as emancipation from individualism, from the isolation of the individual under the conditions of the Western bourgeois society.

Sol Goldberg's photograph of participants in **Allan Kaprow**'s *Women licking jam off of a car*, from his happening *Household* (1964)

Inside and outside views of **Graciela Carnevale**'s action as part of the 'Cycle of Experimental Art', Rosario, Argentina (1968)

CLAIRE BISHOP

So what happens to provocational participation or even "domesticated" participation (as you call it) under regimes other than liberal democracy? In the West, participation is invariably placed in opposition to a society of the spectacle. It is worth comparing it with participatory art in Latin America (under right-wing military dictatorships) and in eastern Europe and Russia (under communism). The examples from Argentina in particular, such as the performances produced by Oscar Masotta and Oscar Bony in Buenos Aires in 1966 and 1968, are quite violent and harbinger more recent work by, say, Santiago Sierra. We could also cite an action by Graciela Carnevale that seems to replicate modes of oppressive social experience that the dictatorship has put in place. Carnevale's action, which took place at the end of the 'Cycle of Experimental Art' in Rosario in 1968, involved locking the viewers in the gallery; she had covered the windows of the space with posters so that they couldn't see out, and walked off with the key. It was then a question of waiting to see what would happen; how would the viewers release themselves from this situation? Carnevale was producing a moment of incarceration which had no clear outcome. Eventually, it was somebody on the outside who broke the window and allowed people to escape, rather than someone on the inside. When I've talked about this piece in public, some audiences have been horrified that an artist would do something this coercive in the context of a series of works of experimental art. In eastern Europe there's a different mode again because of the specific relationship between public and private space and the fact that the work is produced in the context of communism.

BORIS GROYS

… which is a completely different context in which to make art.

CLAIRE BISHOP

The Moscow-based Collective Actions Group (active from 1976 onwards) is a good example of participatory art under communism. Performances usually involved taking a group of spectator-participants out of Moscow on a train for a few hours, to the remote countryside – often to snowy fields that were reminiscent of Malevich's *White Square* paintings. There, some of the participants would be subjected to an enigmatic experience that subsequently became a focus of discussion and analysis by the group. These analyses are gathered together in an eight-volume publication called *Trips to the Countryside*, edited by the main theorist of the group, Andrei Monastyrsky. I know that you took part in a number of these events, such as *The Appearance* (1976), in which the participant-spectators were asked to wait and watch for something to appear in a distant field. Monastyrsky then took a photo of you all watching, and later explained that you had all appeared for him. You argue that these kinds of events create a space of critical distance and spectatorship – in short, a space of liberal democracy – which did not exist under the conditions of communism. Under communism, everyone was a participant, and there was no "outside" space for spectatorship and critical analysis.

BORIS GROYS   I think what should be very clearly said from the beginning is that communism is not a dictatorship. The concept of dictatorship presupposes the existence of a civil society which is independent of the state, which is something other than the state – and is suppressed by the state. In the Soviet Union nobody was suppressed, because everybody was always already a part of the state apparatus. Everybody worked for the state. The relationship between Soviet state and Soviet population was not a political relationship – not even a relationship of political suppression. It was a relationship between employer and employee. That is all. In the Soviet Union to be oppressed one has to create at first the possibility to be oppressed. One has to emancipate oneself to create a different space – outside of the totalitarian space – and then get oppressed. And that is what the participants of the Collective Actions Group did. In this sense the practice of this group is opposite to Western participation art. From Cabaret Voltaire to the happenings of the 1960s, artists tried to escape liberal democracy, individuation, aesthetic distance. It was a desire for totalitarian experience like the Romantic desire of the sublime. But in the case of participation art it is the experience of losing your individuality, dissolving your subjectivity in the ecstatic, Dionysian, totalitarian space – the experience of the political sublime. As Hugo Ball says: "To experience the demise of an individual voice in the general sonoric chaos." Going to these happenings was like going to the Swiss mountains in the nineteenth century. To experience totalitarian frisson, but under the secure conditions of the Western state. In Moscow at the time we were living this frisson all the time. So in this situation one rather tries to construct artificially the position of spectator that does not exist in the society as a whole.

CLAIRE BISHOP   So the Collective Actions Group was trying to construct distance and externality?

BORIS GROYS   To construct distance, construct spectatorship, construct the space of liberal democratic indecision – because the Soviet state was already a huge participatory installation. Inside this space we were trying to create an artificial space of liberal democracy based on the separation between artist and spectator by going to this kind of desert, white desert. So it's space of nothingness. Not part of the state-occupied space. A private space, ultimately. However, it is clear that there is an intimate relationship between destruction and participative art. When a Futurist action destroys art in this traditional form, it also invites all the spectators to participate in this act of destruction, because it does not require any specific artistic skills. In this sense fascism is much more democratic than communism, of course. It is the only thing we can all participate in. So the Western participation art is a manifestation of nostalgia for an impossible dream of total destruction. And at the same time it is an act of total consumption, because the revolution of the 1960s was a revolution of consumption. Consumption is also an act of destruction. And what was a Soviet society? The Soviet society was a society of production without consumption. There was no spectator and no consumer. Everybody was involved in a productive process. So the role of Collective Actions and some other artists of the time was to create the possibility of consumption, the possibility of an external position from which one could enjoy communism. It was not a dissident position, not a position against the Soviet power. Only a very small group of dissidents were really against the Soviet power, but they actually didn't know what to do.

CLAIRE BISHOP   If we are talking about destruction and participation, then a recent work comes to mind, a video by the Polish artist Artur Zmijewski called *Them* (2007). It revolves around a series of painting workshops between four different ideological groups: the young Jews, the young socialists, Polish nationalists and the Catholic church. Each group produces a symbolic image of their beliefs; each image is then amended by the other groups. The only rule of the game is that everyone can interfere with, amend, adjust, or destroy anyone else's image. Needless to say, it ends in complete conflagration, and the final shots show the studio full of smoke and the participants leaving the building. I think Zmijewski does actually want to achieve a progressive space of encounter, but he does this in a perverse way, by making the four groups confront each other. However, it is of course all stage managed – in the style of reality television – so he remains sovereign even though the events are not scripted and it is left open to people to play the game that he sets up.

BORIS GROYS   I think sovereignty is a really relevant word here because the artist-sovereign controls the territory on which this destruction takes place. We have the same thing in the French Revolution, we have the same thing with the Russian Revolution – Robespierre and Lenin controlling the space where the spontaneous collective destruction takes place.

Collective Actions Group's performance *The Appearance* in the country-side outside Moscow (1976)

Still from
Artur
Zmijewski's
Them (2007)

Oleg Kulik's
performance *The
Mad Dog or Last
Taboo Guarded by
Alone Cerber*
(1994)

Maurizio
Cattelan
*Southern
Supplies FC*
(1991)
Colour
photograph,
collage
77×100 cm

CLAIRE BISHOP   Yes. I find it hard to be able to identify what kind of authorship takes place in a work such as Zmijewski's, where an artist sets up the rules of the game and watches it unfold, but without directing the action precisely, where the participants are given some agency. But then, of course, the artist's editing is highly selective. All the footage of the action is recovered into a 30-minute film that has a clear narrative and point of view.

BORIS GROYS   Well, the artist as sovereign, as king, is not meant to do anything. He just symbolises and controls the place where everybody else does something. S/he authorises what these other people are doing. And is the ultimate author.

CLAIRE BISHOP   I think the Italian artist Maurizio Cattelan is another person who is operating within the terms of Futurism today. He provokes and uses the media in a comparable way, although I believe he is lacking the political position that is so important to Futurism. One example is his work called *Southern Supplies FC* (1991). He put together a football team composed entirely of black immigrants and inserted them into a football league. They played matches, but ended up losing every game as they weren't very good. More important than the collaborative aspect of the work, and the use of the real-time system of a football league, is the image that circulates of this all-black Italian football team. This is very ambiguous politically; on the one hand, it's progressive (why not have an all-black football team?), on the other hand, the players are all wearing T-shirts emblazoned with the word *Rauss* (a play on *raus*, the German for "get out"). The word denotes a fictional sponsor, but also tells the uncomfortable truth of what many anti-immigration nationalists might think when seeing the picture. So it's a troubling image that cannot be read clearly one way or another.

BORIS GROYS   We started by saying that the Futurists were extreme, but also very clown-like – and Cattelan fits into this scenario very well. The Futurists didn't have any fear of looking laughable. And it was maybe a real emancipation, because contemporary art became very serious and so concerned with its public image. As well as Cattelan I would also include Oleg Kulik, whose early actions involve behaving like an aggressive dog, biting people and embarrassing them in the street – but being a clown-esque entertainer at the same time. That also reminds me very much of the Futurists.

CLAIRE BISHOP   Yes. But, again, I think the thing that's lacking in all of these examples, which deal with provocation and media attention, is that none is aligned to an identifiable political position.

BORIS GROYS   That's right. I think the connection here is only nostalgic. As I said, it's kind of playing with totalitarian sublime, but with totalitarian sublime that is already not dangerous.

CLAIRE BISHOP   Was Futurism the first of the right-wing avant-gardes?

BORIS GROYS   Well, German Expressionism was partially affiliated to National Socialism in its early days.

CLAIRE BISHOP   It raises the question of which of the array of artistic positions we see around us today, globally, could be considered right-wing – and is the art market?

BORIS GROYS   Liberal democracy and market economy are not right-wing. I think we have to wait for that. Communism was from the beginning not unlike liberal democracy, because both of them are caring about the material wellbeing of people in the first place. That is why the war between them remained the Cold War. To create a true space of political participation one has to sacrifice his privacy – ultimately his life. But who is ready to sacrifice anything at all today? Well, we have that now in Islamic fundamentalism. But in Western culture the tradition of pure sacrifice is predominantly a right-wing fascist tradition – the only alternative to the liberal bio-politics that proclaim life to be of the highest value. In fact, we can see Futurism is a kind of artistic re-enactment of terrorism. There is a long tradition of Italian terrorism actually – from the nineteenth century – as there is a long tradition of Russian terrorism. So that's two cultures where classic terrorism actually emerged, and also was conceptualised. So we can see Russian and Italian Futurism as a kind of nostalgic re-enactment of nineteenth-century terrorism... But against contemporary terrorism the artists have no chance in competition. The Futurists wanted to be like hurricane Katrina – not like a shelter against it. Their every work can be understood as non-constructive, non-objective, senseless. Today, artists complain that they have no practical impact on society, that their projects fail, that they cannot change the world. But, fundamentally, every work is senseless and every project fails. The only difference between artist and non-artist is that the non-artist can not make the failure of his/her project a part of the next project – and the artist can. Art is a wonderful place where you can reflect on the failure of utopia – repeating this failure time and again. It is something that is almost impossible outside of art.

CLAIRE BISHOP   Is it? I'm not sure.

BORIS GROYS   It is. It is impossible because, outside of art, failure has no value. If you fail, you just fail. But in art your failure becomes almost automatically an artistic achievement. At least you can always sell it as such.

CLAIRE BISHOP   Yes, I think that's true. I'm just a little resistant to it, because it sounds too easy.

BORIS GROYS   Yeah, but it also applies to Futurism, because all their actions failed. Neither did they create a new Italy, nor did they create a modern lifestyle...

CLAIRE BISHOP   But they gave momentum to a political project which did achieve changes and which did modernise...

BORIS GROYS   And what happened? Mussolini came to power. And what happened after that? Mussolini failed. And now we don't like Mussolini, but we love Futurism because Futurism was not only a part of the fascist movement, it was also an aesthetic anticipation of the failure of the fascist movement. Futurism already reflected on the clown-esque, the absurdity and senselessness of the fascist action. It already prefigured and reflected on its kitsch aspects and complete ineffectiveness in real life. In this sense, I would say that Futurism created the aesthetics of fascism. At the same time it has shown the impossibility of this aesthetic and anticipated its failure – and that's why we now can love Futurism even if we cannot love fascism.

'Futurism', Tate Modern, 12 June – 20 September, curated by Matthew Gale (head of displays and curator of modern art) with assistant curator Amy Dickson.

Claire Bishop is associate professor in the history of art department at CUNY Graduate Center, New York.

Boris Groys is professor of philosophy and art history at ZKM, Karlsruhe, and global distinguished professor at the NYU, New York.

Filippo Tomasso Marinetti eating spaghetti in the late 1930s

'Futurism', Tate Modern, 12 June – 20 September, curated by Matthew Gale (head of displays and curator of modern art) with assistant curator Amy Dickson.

ACTION FÉMININE

Valentine de
Saint-Point
photographed
by Charles
Reutlinger in
1907

BY ADRIEN SINA & SARAH WILSON

Valentine de Saint-Point (1875–1953), formerly a model for Alphonse Mucha and Rodin, began her life as an artist desired by two important Italian leaders of the avant-garde established in Paris. By 1904 she lived with Ricciotto Canudo, director of the reviews *Europe Artiste* and *Monjoie!* (crucial for Cubist studies) and future author of the *Manifesto of Cerebrist Art*. By 1905 she had met F T Marinetti, director of the review *Poesia* and future author of the *Manifesto of Futurism*. The core of her work was developed in these early years of brainstorming before the explosive period of manifestos from 1909 to 1914. Her thoughts were enriched as she interacted with two visions of modernity: Canudo's, more conceptual, eroticised and sensual, and Marinetti's, more destructive, provocative and energetic. Art historians have never been aware of the importance of this love triangle in the emergence of the avant-gardes. They preserve Marinetti in divine isolation, proclaiming the birth of Futurism as a one-day big bang event that happened on 20 February 1909 and was published in the Parisian newspaper *Le Figaro*.

The theories Saint-Point developed with Canudo through Cerebrism (cerebral + sensual art) were not object-orientated, they were the ultimate level of evolution of the arts after centuries of academic disciplines. This artistic positioning can be better understood today, since we are familiar with disciplines such as Conceptual and Performance art. Her work is marginalised in most exhibitions on Futurism, as they are structured around the hegemony of painting and sculpture. If she is deemed to merit a mention, she is often reduced to an appearance in the chronology, where she is cited in 1912 and 1913 for her *Manifesto of Futurist Women* and her *Futurist Manifesto of Lust*. The ideological rallying cry in the latter, "we must make lust into a work of art", produced no identifiable art object. Rethinking Futurism calls for new curatorial strategies where concept-orientated work can find an adequate space of display.

Art historians note the composition of the *Direction of the Futurist Movement* document, but never notice the real revolutionary aspect contained within it. The statement was divided into five sections: "Poetry", "Painting", "Music", "Sculpture" – all forms of art heavily rooted in the classical past – and then a strange discipline appears on the page, "Action Féminine", represented only by "the poetess Valentine de Saint-Point". We can surmise she invented this notion in contrast to the term feminism, introducing its equivalent into the field of the arts with an innovative and provocative artistic strategy. Establishing this first step, Saint-Point was able to reach realms that no other feminists had done at that time. Reversing centuries of hegemony of the "Spirit" and "Mind", she considered the "Art of Flesh" and the "Art of Lust" to be equally important and anticipated their own field of artistic creation. More than ten years later, her experiments with what would become known as Surrealism, eroticism and sexuality came into their own. Her *Manifesto of Lust* strikingly anticipates key aspects of Surrealism:

"Lust, conceived beyond moral preconceptions and as an essential element of the dynamism of life, is a force."
"Lust is not a sin. Like pride, lust is a virtue that urges one on, an epicentre at which energies are resourced."
"Lust is the expression of a being projected beyond itself."
"Lust is the carnal quest for the unknown."
"Lust is the act of creation and the creation as such."
"Flesh creates as spirit creates. Within the scope of the Universe, their creation is equal. One is not superior to the other, and spiritual creation is not independent from carnal creation."
"We must face lust with awareness. We must make of lust what a refined and intelligent person makes of himself and of his own life, we must make lust into a work of art." – *Futurist Manifesto of Lust*, 1913.

In her early publications *A Love* (1906) and *A Woman and Desire* (1910) Saint-Point explored the feminine psychology of desire, at a time when feminine sexuality was still defined by Freud in terms of "castration" and "lack", compared with male sexuality. In her *Manifesto of Futurist Women* she criticised feminists seeking the same rights as men, arguing that this would lead only to an excess of order, not to the shifts and disorders that Futurists claimed. Instead, she provocatively invited them to be more imaginative, to ask for more unequal rights, even superior or more cruel ones: "Woman, become sublimely unjust once more, like all the forces of nature! Delivered from all control, with your instinct retrieved, you will take your place among the Elements."

The manifesto is structured as a reply to Marinetti's provocation in *Founding Manifesto of Futurism, 1909*: "We wish to glorify War – the only health-giver of the world – militarism, patriotism, the destructive arm of the Anarchist, the beautiful Ideas that kill, the scorn for woman." Saint-Point diplomatically introduces her criticism, explaining that women and men equally deserve the same scorn, that the whole of humanity is becoming mediocre. She also recalls, concerning the issues of war, that woman warriors "fight more ferociously than men", referring to the Amazons, Semiramis or Joan of Arc.

She goes further to set up a broader historical analysis of human civilisations: "It is absurd to divide humanity into men and women. It is only composed of femininity and masculinity." She observes that the periods of history dominated exclusively by masculinity were sterile, brutal and had only wars. The periods dominated exclusively by femininity were turned towards the past and annihilated themselves in fantasies of peace. "The fecund periods, when the most heroes and geniuses come forth from the terrain of culture in all its ebullience, are rich both in masculinity and femininity." After the elaboration of this sensibility of balance and equilibrium, which characterises her thoughts during her whole life, she is back to more supportive sentences for Futurists: "We are living at the end of one of these periods. What is most lacking in women as in men is virility. That is why Futurism, even with all its exaggerations, is right." But this support publicly ended in 1914 when she left the movement and its violence.

She had already analysed the psychology of violence and excess within the terms of an eroticised and sexualised political power, in her modern tragedy *The Imperial Soul - The Agony of Messalina*. This play was staged in 1908 and then published with a statement of theory in 1926. An intimate landscape of lust, force, desire and despair is depicted through the powerful words of the Empress during her death agony:

"Once more I will see you pale from voluptuousness
Or from the obscure desire of my hot beauty
Once more I will exhaust your sons, your brothers,
Your lovers, your husbands!
My insatiable flesh still reigns over all…"

As an aspect of her "Art of Flesh" Saint-Point initiated a new cross-media performative form of art that she called "metachory", a combination of Greek words meaning beyond the dance. The first metachory was staged in Paris in 1913, with a theoretical explanation, after which she performed a solo almost naked, her body partly veiled by transparent silk strips. Her face was veiled in order to focus the audience's attention on the abstract and geometrical aspects of her dances and not on emotions, since Futurists rejected sentimentality. Her movements were combined with words from her *Poems of War and Love*, light projections of mathematical equations and an effusion of perfumes. The music was disconnected from the gestures. As opposed to other dancers of her epoch, such as Loie Fuller or Isadora Duncan, she wanted neither dance that expressed the emotions of the music, nor music that expressed the emotions of dance. She separated them as two autonomous layers in interaction, anticipating the experiments of composer John Cage and choreographer Merce Cunningham years later in America in the 1950s. Innovative composers who created music for her included Claude Debussy, Roland Manuel, Dane Rudhyar, Erik Satie, Maurice Droeghmans and the Futurist Francesco Balilla Pratella. The Metachory Festival she staged in 1917 at the Metropolitan Opera House, New York, introduced American audiences to her polytonal and dissonant music.

In the later period of Futurism, Marinetti extended his lyricism of war to the support of fascism and his friendship with Mussolini. Saint-Point developed several unrealised political projects, including the collaboration entitled the "United States of Mediterranea". She left France for Egypt in 1924, shortly after the death of Canudo. As an ultimate form of artistic positioning and feminine action, she bravely initiated political actions in Cairo against war, colonialism and injustice. Harassed by both French and British intelligence services, she was obliged to stop the publication of her review *Le Phoenix* (1925–1927), which tried to reunite Christian and Islamic civilisations through art and culture. Her book *The Truth about Syria* (1929) contained an accurate geopolitical vision, anticipating the

tragedy we are now witnessing in Palestine and Lebanon. In 1933 she functioned as a mediator in peace discussions between France and Syria – before the French army launched an attack that ended in a disastrous defeat. Valentine de Saint-Point died in Cairo in 1953, disillusioned but peaceful, inspired by the mystical serenity of Sufism and the desert. She lived her final years as a modern Lady Hester Stanhope, who, ironically, had caught the eye of Saint-Point's ancestor, the French poet, politician and pacifist revolutionary Alphonse de Lamartine. His castle was situated in the village of Saint-Point, from which Valentine took her surname.

Feminine Futures, *dedicated to Valentine de Saint-Point and edited by Adrien Sina, is forthcoming from Presses du Réel. The exhibition 'Feminine Futures' will be part of the PERFORMA Biennale, New York, in November. A selection of archival material relating to Valentine de Saint-Point is included in 'Futurism', Tate Modern.*

Adrien Sina *is a curator and theoretician, and "thinker in residence" at the Live Art Development Agency, London.*

Sarah Wilson *is reader in the history of modern and contemporary art at the Courtauld Institute, where she teaches courses on performance art. She co-curated the 'Pierre Klossowski and The Vicious Circle' exhibition at the Whitechapel Art Gallery, London, in 2006.*

Valentine de Saint-Point (centre) with theatre director Vivian Dumas (left) and music director Rudyard Chennevierre (right), New York (1917)

Title page of
**Valentine de
Saint-Point**'s
*Futurist
Manifesto of
Lust* (1913)

Title page of
**Valentine de
Saint-Point**'s
Un Amour (1906)

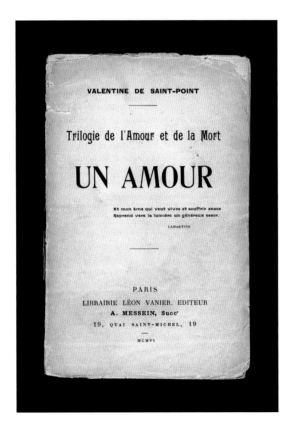

'Action Féminine'

Field Visit: Armin Linke

Armin Linke
Three Gorges Dam,
Yichang (Hupeh)
China (1998)
C-type print
150×200 cm

Armin Linke
Ghazi Barotha hydroelectric
scheme, workers praying
Hattian, Pakistan (1999)
C-type print
150×200 cm

THE HISTORY

Armin Linke
Star City ZPK,
Moscow, Russia (1998)
C-type print
150×200 cm

Armin Linke
Polar Cap,
Arctic North Pole (2001)
C-type print
150×200 cm

OF NOW

BY KURT W FORSTER

Armin Linke has a studio in a humdrum part of Milan, but if one wishes to do more than catch a glimpse of this peripatetic photographer, one needs to travel with him. He packs his bags whenever something grabs his attention. At first this has nothing to do with the camera, but everything to do with his eye and a disarming intelligence. Linke quietly scrutinises his chosen location, selecting a view that is of a scope and depth to warrant taking a picture. One day in Iraq, before the last war, he did just that, some distance from one of Saddam Hussein's palaces on a slope of asphalt and sand. While he set up his camera, a group of men uniformly dressed in black walked into his view. They were leaving the palace after bearing birthday wishes for the president. The resulting photograph is really composed of two images: one is premeditated, taking in the sweep of a symbolic site (with few or no symbols, apart from the tall lamp posts, as if it were an airport); the other is created by coincidence. It is precisely the accidental that endows the picture with an uncanny meaning: men are leaving the site of power, as if the place were to fall vacant at their departure. By dint of its dual nature, the image enfolds a brief moment within a static frame. Linke caught an instant (gone the moment he snapped the picture) whose symbolic time had not yet come, but whose enduring backdrop ceased to hold any significance. Instead of fading into obsolete reportage as the years go by, the picture continues to acquire incalculable references.

Linke has a keen eye for places on the verge of historical change or in the throes of transformation. Gigantic construction sites, mining pits and hydroelectric dams figure among his growing inventory of images, to which we can add polar regions, Soviet cosmodromes and Chinese cities. In these pictures, the photographer's gaze remains steady, even unblinking, taking no umbrage and making no excuses.

The sheer vastness of some of the locations is matched by their emptiness, by the fleeting presence of workmen in the far distance, or by a thin plume of dust as the only sign of human transience. An overwhelming discrepancy of scale, often under unstable skies, causes doubt about what one sees. Can it be true? What if one actually were in such a place?

Because Linke retouches his pictures only in the rarest of circumstances, digitally dampening brightness or enhancing the howling desert of polar ice, they look compelling. He remains a staunch opportunist in his conviction that photographs achieve their character as a record of sites and occurrences rather than through the artifice of the photographer. He eschews shallow depths of field such as Gabriele Basilico has recently imposed on his urban landscapes, and he would never edit his photographs in the calculated way that Andreas Gursky manipulates and inflates his images to almost hypnotic effect. Linke remains a reporter at heart, attuned to occasions and prepared for their disruptive moment.

As we drive up the Brenner Pass, on our way to the inauguration of the new Museum of Modern and Contemporary Art in Bolzano, we ascend into a pocket of Italy that belongs to both northern and southern Europe, harbouring palm trees and lush gardens at the foot of snowcapped mountains, a hybrid world in which everything carries two names, one in Italian, the other in German. Linke, a German who grew up in Italy, should feel perfectly at home in this region. He left art school early and moved to New York, where he found himself on the scene of artists and literati whose pictures he snapped as if he were compiling an album of his workaday experiences. *Casa Vogue* discovered his cache and kept him busy with requests for more. The reporter in him was awakened

Giovanni Segantini's
Death (1898–1899)
from the *Alpen Triptych*
Oil on canvas
190×322cm

Film stills from
Armin Linke's
video installation
Alpi Film Project (2008)

'The History of Now'

and nurtured in the hothouse of galleries and fashion magazines.

Linke knows that for a photograph to warrant more than the lightning response we're accustomed to according it, the image must hold something that we sense but cannot necessarily see. Only pictures that arrest the viewer's attention can escape automatic dispatch. This resistance may be fragile, but it needs to be obstinate. On the one hand, the unfamiliar may prompt us to look more closely; on the other, what we already know may hol d even more of a mystery when it is rendered anew. Linke has taken many memorable photographs in both of these categories: the ramshackle cabins in which Russian cosmonauts changed into their space gear suggest booths in a discount clothing store; Pakistani construction workers praying during their night shift under the glare of lights at the foot of a concrete dam could not have been watched with more respect, but also with an unyielding will to observe.

On the way back south, we drive up the Engadine valley where resorts bristle with hotels jumbling together ostentatious palace architecture with half-timbered chalets. Chic shopping arcades and rustic hostels for alpinists alternate with sites of literary and artistic lore. While Marcel Proust journeyed to the coast of Normandy, Friedrich Nietzsche and Giovanni Segantini sought out the bracing alpine landscapes. To this day, travellers match their mental pictures of the valleys with present-day reality, remaining baffled as often as elated. Where Dr Moriarty and Sherlock Holmes plunged to their deaths, or where Nietzsche beheld a midnight vision of fated returns, four and five-star hotels beckon tourists to the edge of the abyss and induce a faint frisson of the sublime. We cast only a strafing glance up at the fake chateau of Zuoz with its wing recently designed by Ben van Berkel as a crystalline object of intriguing nature. Driving on to St Moritz, we make an obligatory stop, not only to acquire confections of nut and pear cake, but most of all to spend a quiet moment contemplating Segantini's panoramic triptych *Life, Nature, Death* (1896–1899). For the price of a cinema ticket, one can witness these truly cinematic paintings from the turn of the century inside a rotunda in St Moritz's Segantini Museum. Three wide canvases open up magnificent views whose differences carry an urgent sense of the passage of time and the fragility of life.

Segantini's triptych was in Linke's mind when he conceived the three-screen projection of still and moving images for the Venice Biennale of 2003. The project, made in collaboration with artist/composer Renato Rinaldi and architect Piero Zanini, did not end there, and is now taking on new dimensions. Linke has been preparing an Alpen film symphony of his own – an ongoing pictorial documentation of the Alps – with Nietzschean overtones: short cinematic scenes caption sublime settings with everyday experiences, such as military manoeuvres, shepherds leading their flocks, meteorological simulations with dry ice and skiers storming the highest peaks in mechanical

conveyances. At the time when our assault on the Alps renders the livelihood of its seasoned inhabitants ever more precarious, the lowlanders arrive in droves for simulated snowfalls, artificial cascades and night-time skiing. An episode on top of one of Europe's tallest mountains baffles by its near-invisibility: tourists staggering through thick blankets of fog, careering over snowy slopes and posing for pictures in which there will be nothing but veils of white and spectral shadows. As if the camera were the only instrument to fix an evanescent moment of experience, everyone is wielding one, and Linke was on site to observe – with his – the uselessness of everyone else's.

On the way down to Milan, we spend a moment in the cemetery at the Church of San Giorgio in Borgonovo in the Bregaglia valley to visit the tombs of the Giacometti family: a boulder smoothed down by Alberto for the grave of his father Giovanni, and little more than a slab of granite set up by Diego for his brother, but vandalised and now bearing flowers and pebbles left by visitors. Alberto transformed a stone from the nearby river bed into a torso, raising shallow shapes of sun and moon and a bird from its surface. As we bend over the boulder, the sun is setting behind the peaks. Giacometti's torso is already sinking into uncanny twilight. Only by running one's hand over the stone, still warm from the day's heat, can one feel the irregularities of its shape. Water and wind have worn its surface; lichens have spread yellowish blotches over it. We sense, like a cold exhalation, the geology of time. The rapid eclipse of sunlight darkens the bottom of the valley under a radiant sky.

For several years Armin Linke has fashioned a series of simultaneous episodes that momentarily expand into panoramic continuity, thereby eluding our visual grasp, and sudden plunges into depth – like ski jumpers descending the launch ramp. Lateral expanse and focused depth imply different times of experience and combine to build the several rhythms of his images. These pictures move even when they are still, and they muffle the swish of time, although we hear clanking cowbells or the crashing sound of falling rock. Life is made of noise and rush alternating with uncanny moments of stillness and loss. Linke has found a way of bringing them into view without allowing time to shred his images. In an embrace as astonishing as it is spontaneous, he matches fleeting moments with the watchful permanence of pyramids.

Armin Linke is showing as part of 'YOU[ser]: Das Jahrhundert des Konsumenten' at the ZKM Museum Für Neue Kunst & Mediamuseum in Karlsruhe, Germany, until 31 August, and at Museum für Gegenwartskunst, Siegen, 27 May – 20 September.

Kurt W Forster is Scully professor of the history of architecture at Yale University. His most recent publication is the introduction to Building a New Europe: Portraits of Modern Architects, Essays by George Nelson, 1935–36 _(Yale University Press, 2007, in association with the School of Architecture)._

Film stills from
Armin Linke's
video installation
Alpi Film Project (2008)

'The History of Now'

BY ROBERT MACFARLANE

FIVE, SIX, PICK UP STICKS

Richard Long
outside St Martin's
School of Art,
London, at the
start of *Cycling
Sculpture*, *1-3
December 1967*

Courtesy the artist. Photograph: Oded Hallamny

Richard Long
*A Night of Rain
Sleeping Place
An 8 Day
Mountain Walk
in Sobaeksan
Korea Spring
1993* (1993)
Photograph

In 1980 Richard Long exhibited at the newly opened Anthony d'Offay Gallery in Dering Street, London. The show was mixed-media: maps and photographs recorded a *Water Circle Walk* made between four lochs in the Scottish Highlands; terse text notes detailed *Two Straight Twelve Mile Walks on Dartmoor*; and across the floor of the gallery stretched *Somerset Willow Line*, hundreds of barkless willow batons laid out in the form of a section of path, 16½ metres long and two metres wide. An allusion, in part, to the Sweet Track – the causeway of bound coppice poles that was built around 3800 BC in order to give safe passage across the swampy Somerset Levels.

Unexpectedly, the d'Offay show was accompanied by a "Statement" from Long. Unexpectedly – because Long had previously kept silent on the subject of his own work, preferring to exhibit it unglossed. Printed at the Curwen Press, it appeared on a single sheet of card, folded into three panels. Its title was "Five, six, pick up sticks, seven, eight, lay them straight", and the text consisted of 44 sentences, laid out on the page almost as the stanzas of a poem. The simplicity and repetitions of his language (as seen in the fragments below), combined with the *mise en page*, gave the document a peculiar atmosphere: part Ten

Commandments, part nursery rhyme –

*I like the simplicity of walking,
the simplicity of stones.*

*I like common means given
the simple twist of art.*

I choose lines and circles because they do the job.

*My art is about working in the wide world,
wherever, on the surface of the earth.*

*My work is not urban, nor is it romantic.
It is the laying down of modern ideas
in the only practical places to take them.*

You might be able to hear the rasp of annoyance in that last section. For Long had been provoked to issue his statement out of irritation – irritation at the persistent mischaracterisation of his work as "romantic", and irritation at finding himself repeatedly placed in a tradition of reverie-minded walker-philosophers that started with Rousseau and marched through Wordsworth, Coleridge, Borrow and

Richard Long's
Walking Man
and *Plaster
Path* at the
West of
England
College of Art,
Bristol (1965)

Thoreau. This was an attempt to clarify his methods
and his ambitions.

Long's impatience seems to me quite understandable:
romantic walking is so clearly a false genealogy for his art.
The British version of this tradition is filled with pedestrians
(William Hazlitt, Robert Louis Stevenson, Edward Thomas)
who wish to stride back into a true sense of themselves.
They foot forwards into the metaphysical wind of the world,
letting it scour away the sour accretions of life – and
they end their walks stripped back to their ideal natures.
By contrast, American romantic roadsters (Henry David
Thoreau, Ralph Waldo Emerson, John Muir) are more
anticipatory: they imagine the walk as a way to find a new
self, rather than to retrieve a lost one. British walkers
recover, American walkers discover – and both traditions
celebrate a self-consciousness on the part of the walker.
They cherish the walker as thinker, and the walker as talker.

Either way, these walkers have very little in common
with Long, who has always been far less interested in
reflection than in motion, and less in mind than in body.
His art practises, in fact, an almost immodest discretion
with regard to the ego. The marks he has left behind in
landscapes – rock-rows, snow-drawings, trails of crushed
grass, circles of slate-blades – appear to be the scrupulously
anonymised traces of an unspecific human body moving
through space and time. That said, to describe his work as
egoless isn't to declare it devoid of personal content. And
one of the most intriguing aspects of his art is how subtly
it registers and re-expresses aspects of his childhood.
Michael Craig-Martin, reviewing the d'Offay show for
The Burlington Magazine, noticed this: "The art is rooted
in his home territory and his childhood experience."
Long later confirmed Craig-Martin's intuition. "I feel
I carry my childhood with me in lots of aspects of my work,"
he remarked. "Why stop skimming stones when you
grow up?"

Why indeed? It's a lovely question – innocently
seen and innocently phrased. And Long has never stopped
skimming stones, artistically speaking. His hundreds
of circles – made around the world in stone, sand, wood,
grass and footprints – can be imagined as the ripples
of these skimmed stones. To my mind, his work is best
understood as a set of persistently childish acts: the
outcomes of a brilliantly unadulterated being-in-the-world.

The word kindergarten was coined in 1840 by the
German educationalist Friedrich Froebel (1782–1852).
Kindergarten, literally "a children's garden": a school or space
for early learning. Froebel (less remembered now than
Maria Montessori or Rudolf Steiner, for he didn't lend his
name to his method) wanted to create an environment
in which children could be childish in the best sense
of that word. Banished from his kindergartens was the
Gradgrindian sense of the infant as a vessel to be filled
with facts. Instead, he fostered an ideal of the child as
micronaut – an explorer of the world's textures, laws and
frontiers, who should be left to make his or her own

Richard Long
walking on
Dartmoor with his
father (1968)

Richard Long
standing in
the viewing
place of
England 1967,
at Ashton
Park, Bristol
(1967)

'Five, Six, Pick Up Sticks'

discoveries through unstructured play. Froebel wanted children to "reach out and take the world by the hand, and palpate its natural materials and laws", as Marina Warner observes in a fine essay on play, "to discover gravity and grace, pliancy and rigidity, to sense harmonies and experience limits".

A nature-lover and walker from an early age, Froebel had a passion for the patterns of phenomena, and in particular for what he called "the deeper lying unity of natural objects". It was for this reason that the early Froebelian kindergartens had few figurative toys. Instead of trains, dolls and knights, there were wooden cubes and spheres, coloured squares and circles, pebbles, shells and pick-up-sticks. Children spent their days singing songs and playing games, arranging the pebbles in spirals and circles, balancing blocks and picking up sticks. This open play was, as Froebel imagined it, the means by which "the child became aware of itself, and its place within the universe".

Long is a childish artist in the Froebelian sense, and the wild world is his kindergarten. When Clarrie Wallis, curator of the new Tate exhibition, observes that his work is about his "own physical engagement, exploring the order of the universe and nature's elemental forces… about measuring the world against ourselves", she could be describing the Froebelian method. For more than 40 years Long has been using his moving body to explore limits, sense harmonies and apprehend balance and scale. His materials and his vocabulary have always been uncomplicated and childish. "I am content with the vocabulary of universal and common means," he wrote quietly in 1982, "walking, placing, stones, sticks, water, circles, lines, days, nights, roads." Again in 1985: "My pleasure is in walking, lifting,

placing, carrying, throwing, marking." In 1968 he showed a sculpture of sticks cut from trees along the Avon and laid end to end in lines on the gallery floor. Five, six, pick up sticks. Seven, eight, lay them straight.

"A walk," wrote Long in 1980, "is just one more layer, a mark." Children, like Long, are passionate mark-makers. As any parent knows, a child is happiest when playing with surfaces that record its passage or presence. Ice-lidded puddles that smash like mirrors or crockery. Leaf-drifts that scuff and kick into clouds. A crayon scrawled along a white wall (a line taken for a walk). A stick dragged along railings, leaving its steam-engine sound-trail behind it. Dirty shoes tracking footprints across a kitchen floor.

Long's first landscape work, *Snowball Track* (1964), occurred when he rolled up a snowball, and then photo-graphed the wobbly dark path of revealed grass left by it. In 1970 at the Dwan Gallery he wore muddy boots and stomped a spiral of smeared dirt on to the floor, the uncoiled length of which corresponded to a straight climb that he had previously made from the bottom to the top of Silbury Hill in Wiltshire. This was among the first of Long's many daub-works from the 1970s, which he made by using his feet or hands to wipe, smudge, blotch and spread mud and soil on to the floor. Seeing black-and-white images of these works now, they resemble evolved versions of the hand-prints left by the Lascaux Cave artists around 17,000 years ago – or of a child's first prints in mud or paint. Ontogeny recapitulating phylogeny.

When he was growing up, Long was lucky enough to be indulged in his compulsive mark-making. His parents let him draw all over his bedroom walls, creating a mural-in-progress. At the age of five he negotiated with his primary school headmistress over whether he could miss morning service if he spent the hour painting instead (his negotiations were successful). In 1966, while still an art student, he persuaded his neighbour to allow him to incise a work called *Turf Circle* into his manicured back lawn.

The lines of continuity from Long's childhood into his adult work are multiple and clear. "My father used to take us down to see the spring tides [of the River Avon]," he recalled. "I grew up playing on the tow-path… when I was a child I just used to find the River Avon a great place. And children are no intellectuals. They just play in the places which are nice to be in. So all my fascination with water, the roots of my art, developed in my childhood." The puddle splash, the muddy stick, the two-footed jump, fingers drawing pictures in the dust – how strongly those early river days have leaked into his later art. In the 1980s he extended his repertoire of daub-works, transferring them from floor to wall, and exploring new patterns and forms. He began to use his right hand as the brush: dipping it in a bucket of mud, then wiping the mud on to the wall to create splash paintings, then allowing the silt to drain down and disperse its alluvial deposits, forming arbitrary fans and deltas. The mud that Long uses most often for this work comes from the Avon, which he claims produces the most artistically helpful mud in the world, in terms of its adhesiveness and texture.

Lynne Cooke, in a 1983 essay that stung Long sharply, described his text-works as "wilfully precious", and compared his photographs with colonial "trophies". His art, she wrote, exerts a "powerful hegemony" (this at a time when the word hegemony was thrown around rather more often in art criticism than it is today). Long "attempts to order the world", she wrote, "he… imposes order on nature". But Cooke got Long wrong. He's no hegemonist, nor an imposer of order. Rather, he is a discoverer of order, an experimenter in limit and form. A *homo ludens*, to borrow the title of Johann Huizinga's synoptic 1938 study

of the play-impulse, which so influentially connected play and art.

Long the solemn child, then, whose work recalls Melanie Klein's definition of play as "a serious form of meaning-making – often compulsive, repetitive and anxious". And, in this respect, he can usefully be connected with those artists who have seen the walk as play (which is quite different from seeing the walk as comedy). He can be placed in the company of, say, Bruce Nauman, whose 1967–1968 video performance piece *Walking in an Exaggerated Manner, around the Perimeter of a Square* shows Nauman placing his feet – with the amplified care of a tightrope-walker teetering leagues above a city street – along the edge of a taped square in a room. And he can, perhaps, share at least imaginative space with Watt, the eponymous character of Samuel Beckett's third novel, whose "way of advancing due east" (wrote Beckett with playful seriousness in or around 1942) "was to turn his bust as far as possible towards the north and at the same time to fling out his right leg as far as possible towards the south, and then to turn his bust as far as possible towards the south and at the same time to fling out his left leg as far as possible towards the north".

'Richard Long: Heaven and Earth', supported by the Richard Long Exhibition Supporters Group and The Henry Moore Foundation, Tate Britain, 2 June – 6 September, curated by Clarrie Wallis, curator of contemporary British art, Tate Britain, with Helen Little, assistant curator. Richard Long: Heaven and Earth, *including essays by Clarrie Wallis, Nicholas Serota and Andrew Wilson and a conversation between Richard Long and Michael Craig-Martin, is published by Tate Publishing.*

Robert Macfarlane is the author of Mountains of the Mind *and* The Wild Places *(both Granta) and is currently writing* The Old Ways, *a book about paths and walking to be published by Hamish Hamilton. A BBC adaptation of* The Wild Places, *set in Essex, is screened next year.*

Still from **Bruce Nauman's** *Walking in an Exaggerated Manner around the Perimeter of a Square* (1968) 16mm black-and-white film, silent, 10 minutes

'Five, Six, Pick Up Sticks'

Richard Long
Campsite Stones
Sierra Nevada
1985 (1985)
Photograph

'Five, Six, Pick Up Sticks'

"I ENVY HIS GIFT OF BEING ABLE TO WALK INTO A PATCH OF WOODS AND EMERGE WITH THE MAKINGS OF A GREAT INSTALLATION FROM AN ARM FULL OF TWIGS"

BY CARL ANDRE

Untitled (Portrait of Richard Long) made from sticks given by Long to **Carl Andre** and photographed by Andre (1969)

I first encountered Richard Long's work in Konrad Fischer's gallery in Düsseldorf. I was at once surprised and disturbed by the installation of pine needles on the floor of the gallery. I said: "Konrad, you can't make art out of pine needles." Konrad said: "You can now." When I saw it I, and everyone else, looked down on it and rejoiced.

As for the story of how *Portrait of Richard Long* came about… At the age of 73, I find that my memory has become unreliable in so far as it exists at all. As I recall, Frank Stella made a series of witty portraits of friends and acquaintances in the form of strip drawings and paintings. In response, I made a series of small, improvised floor sculptures as portraits of my friends. I think I took my portrait of Richard to Cornell University (where he was exhibiting in 'From Earth Art to Eco Art') as a gift for him.

Richard once said: "I like simple, practical, emotional, quiet, vigorous art." I would agree with his list, except I would substitute the word "passionate" for the word

"emotional". Of course artworks cannot possess emotions, but I do respond passionately to Richard's work. From his art I feel a "fierce calm". I envy his gift of being able to walk into a patch of woods and emerge with the makings of a great installation from an arm full of twigs.

Richard's work has inspired me in many different ways. I am not at all tempted to imitate him – our gifts and sensibilities are much too different to allow for that. His standards are so high I have no choice but to demand more of myself. I am sure I am a better artist for having met Richard and his work, and I have always enjoyed his subtle and piercing wit. I have never met an artist finer than Richard, nor a man of higher standards or better character than he.

Carl Andre is an artist based in New York. His exhibition at Sadie Coles HQ, London, runs from 15 July to 22 August.

Colour Chart I: Tate Liverpool's exhibition 'Colour Chart: Reinventing Colour, 1950 to Today' explores the moment in twentieth-century art when a group of artists began to perceive colour as "readymade" rather than purely scientific or expressive. The gallery's director talks to one of its leading practitioners

Ellsworth Kelly
Méditerranée
(1952)
Oil on nine
joined wood
panels, three
in relief
150.5×193.7×7cm

Ellsworth Kelly
*Colors for a Large
Wall* (1951)
Oil on canvas
mounted on 64
joined panels
240×240cm

SIXTY YEARS AT FULL INTENSITY

Ellsworth Kelly
Spectrum I (1953)
Oil on canvas
152.4×152.4cm

BY CHRISTOPH GRUNENBERG & ELLSWORTH KELLY

CHRISTOPH GRUNENBERG

In 1951 you did a number of paintings with random arrangements of bright colours. These works, in particular *Colors for a Large Wall* (1951), were a radical departure from your previous, mostly figurative paintings and from the collages experimenting with abstraction derived from observed phenomena of the visible world. Can you describe their genesis?

ELLSWORTH KELLY

In October 1951 I left Paris and went to the south of France. The summer before, observing how light fragmented on the surface of water, I painted *Seine*, made of black and white rectangles arranged by chance. I then started a series of eight collages titled *Spectrum Colors Arranged by Chance I* to *VIII*. Before this I had not used colour extensively. The collages employed different systems and arrangements, using chance to organise where a spectrum of eighteen colours would be placed.

Ellsworth Kelly
*Spectrum Colors
Arranged by
Chance II* (1951)
Collage on paper
97.2×97.2cm

CHRISTOPH GRUNENBERG

Did you use a mathematical system with the early works?

ELLSWORTH KELLY

It was a chance system for the placement of colours on a grid. Numbered slips of paper each referred to a colour, one of eighteen different hues to be placed on a grid 40 inches by 40 inches. Each of the eight collages used a different process.

CHRISTOPH GRUNENBERG

Did you make conscious references in the arrangement of these works to the aesthetics of the colour chart?

ELLSWORTH KELLY

I never thought of colour charts at all when I was working on them. They were really an experiment. I wanted to show how any colour goes with any other colour. Above all, I wanted to learn about colour relationships. Many of the works of this period start from chance encounters, such as shadows on a staircase, the reflections of the sun on the River Seine and the exposed sides of buildings that showed the abstract black patterns where the chimneys had been. After the experiments with arranging colours by chance came my first works using the actual colour spectrum as a source (*Spectrum I*, 1953).

CHRISTOPH GRUNENBERG

Did finding those coloured papers in Paris help you to reach abstraction?

ELLSWORTH KELLY

I used them as an indication for the hue, as a guide only. When I painted I always mixed the colours that I wanted; all were bright and at their full intensity.

Ellsworth Kelly
*Red Yellow Blue
White* (1952)
Dyed cotton on
25 panels in
five parts
Each panel
152.4×30.5cm

CHRISTOPH GRUNENBERG

Was there something about the light, the atmosphere and intensity of colour that was reflected in those compositions made in Paris and in the south of France?

ELLSWORTH KELLY

While working in Paris after the war everything was grey and, as I've said, I used very little colour. When I finally went to Sanary, I did *Colors for a Large Wall*. It was the first work I painted in the south of France.

CHRISTOPH GRUNENBERG

How did you come to execute *Colors for a Large Wall* in separate panels?

ELLSWORTH KELLY

Having done the collages and worked with the individual colour squares helped me to see that I could use a different canvas on its own stretcher for each of the 64 panels that make up *Colors for a Large Wall*. Each would have only one colour. This dispensed with the problem of composition, of internal divisions of the canvas. The division was a given of the material support, not something drawn on it.

CHRISTOPH GRUNENBERG   Was this transcending of the canvas the beginning of the idea of the mural, which you were very interested in at the time?

ELLSWORTH KELLY   In the 1960s the Minimalists' work was considered to be more or less what it is. The painting or sculpture represents itself. I feel that ten years earlier, starting in 1950, I was struggling with exactly the same problem. *Colors for a Large Wall* constructed of 64 separate panels becomes a "painting object" that separates the form – the painting – and the ground, which becomes the wall. The edge of one panel next to another panel is not the same as one colour painted next to another colour on a single canvas. When I want to do a painting with one colour overlapping another, it has to be a real overlap, not a depicted overlap. I didn't want to paint an overlap, meaning that it would be a deception or illusion. I no longer wanted to depict space, but to make a work that existed in literal space. Thus, my recent works are one canvas as a relief over another canvas. Another important example of a panel painting that explores the idea of the mural was *Red Yellow Blue White* (1952). It's the only one I ever did using actual dyed fabric of ready-made colours, which moves the painting into the realm of real objects. It consists of five vertical panels, each with five canvases. The vertical panels are separated on the wall and the intervals of the wall surface between them are part of the painting.

CHRISTOPH GRUNENBERG   Do you think the relief paintings, such as *Méditerranée* (1952), are coming more out of the early relief works, or out of the multi-panel ones such as *Colors for a Large Wall*?

ELLSWORTH KELLY   Both. Relief work figures predominantly during my time in Paris. After *Méditerranée*, the pictures were mainly paintings in multiple panels.

CHRISTOPH GRUNENBERG   How did your use of colour differ between France and the United States?

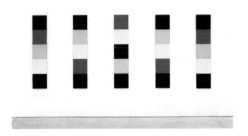

ELLSWORTH KELLY   In Europe at the beginning of the twentieth century, the Fauves – Matisse, Derain – were using bright colours in their full intensity, which continued with Kandinsky, Malevich, Kirchner, Léger and Mondrian. They employed all the colours of the spectrum. In the 1940s and 1950s the majority of the Abstract Expressionists in New York rebelled against this European use of colour and mostly used mixed colours. That is, the Abstract Expressionists did use bright colours sometimes, but they tended to paint wet-on-wet, which muddled their hues. As Matisse would say, a small patch of any one colour is far less intense than a large one of the same colour. I returned in 1954 to New York and showed paintings done in France at the Betty Parsons Gallery in 1956 with bright colours that wouldn't really be used until the Pop artists in the 1960s. My idea of using colour at its full intensity, which began with *Colors for a Large Wall*, hasn't changed in the 60 years that I've been painting.

'Colour Chart: Reinventing Colour, 1950 to Today', Tate Liverpool, 29 May – 13 September, was curated by Ann Temkin, chief curator of painting and sculpture at the Museum of Modern Art, New York. At Tate Liverpool the exhibition is organised by Christoph Grunenberg, director, and Sook-Kyung Lee, exhibitions and displays curator. The catalogue Colour Chart: Reinventing Colour, 1950 to Today is published by the Museum of Modern Art, New York.

Christoph Grunenberg is the director of Tate Liverpool.

Ellsworth Kelly is an artist based in New York.

A BIT OF NOTHING

BY DAVID BATCHELOR

My original motives for making monochromes – back in the late 1980s – were vaguely malicious. The subject was interesting because it seemed to be pretty much the dumbest kind of painting that it is possible to make. A single uninterrupted plane of flat unmodulated colour spread evenly across a given surface – a monochrome appears to involve no composition, no drawing, no subtlety; and it requires no skill, and certainly no craft skill, to make one. Anyone who can paint a door can paint a monochrome. Or, as El Lissitzky put it in 1925: "Now the production of art has been simplified to such an extent that one can do no better than order one's paintings by telephone from a house painter while one is lying in bed." This was painting as low comedy, the *reductio ad absurdum* of high abstraction. Having said that, a part of what attracted me to the monochrome was also the awareness that for many artists this form of painting had promised a great deal more – the freeing of colour from the tyranny of line, the liberation of painting from the register of representation and the possibility of a brush with some sublime void or other metaphysical nothingness. It's just that I didn't believe that anyone could still seriously maintain its claims to transcendence, be they formal, spiritual or otherwise.

So there was the monochrome: born in revolution (around 1920, say, in the tussles between Malevich, Rodchenko, Lissitzky and others); grown through tricky adolescence to some kind of ambiguous respectability in the 1950s and 1960s (think Yves Klein, Piero Manzoni, Lucio Fontana in Europe; Ad Reinhardt, Robert Rauschenberg, Ellsworth Kelly in the US; Hélio Oiticica in Brazil, etc.); and now old, fat and bloated, come to die as corporate decoration in the boardrooms and marble foyers of every other steel and glass office block, hanging over the head of the CEO like a halo, only rectangular and usually grey. At least, that's what I thought, back then. In truth it was difficult to think of that many actual corporate monochromes, but I loved the image none the less and that, for a while, was good enough for me.

The monochromes I started making began life as paintings, gradually turned into reliefs and then, after a few years of flailing around, ended up on the floor as objects. The first ones were black. They turned white over time, became silver for a while and occasionally went red – out of embarrassment I suspect. And all the while there was this nagging question: if the monochrome was so simple, why was this all taking so long? In retrospect, I realise

 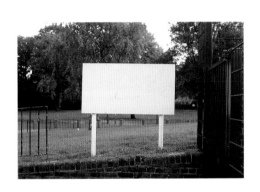 

David Batchelor photographs (top, left to right): *Stratford, London, 10.03.04*; *Stoke Newington, 20.09.02*; *Islington, London, 01.05.09*. Middle, left to right: *Elephant and Castle, London, 20.02.98*; *Victoria Park, London, 23.11.08*; *Quinta Normal, Santiago, Chile, 31.03.05*. Bottom, left to right: *Alexanderplatz, Berlin, 04.04.08*; *Ponte Lungo, Rome, 17.04.07*; *King's Cross, London, 18.11.07*

'A Bit of Nothing'

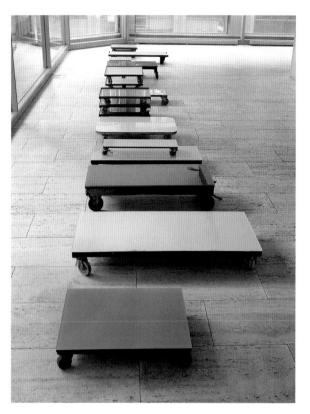

David Batchelor
*I Love King's Cross and King's
Cross Loves Me* (1996-1997)
Found dollies, acrylic sheet,
enamel paint
Dimensions variable

Yves Klein
*Untitled
Monochrome Blue
IKB 67* (1959)
Oil on canvas
92×73cm

On Kawara
May 25, 1966
From *Today Series,
No. 89*, "A rocket
scientist was killed
by a foreign-made
.25 caliber pistol,
Columbus, Ohio."* (1966)
Liquitex on canvas
25.4×33cm

Robert Rauschenberg
*Untitled (Small Black
Painting)* (1953)
Oil and newspaper on
canvas
55.9×71.1cm

one of my many difficulties was I had an idea of what I wanted without any obvious sense of what these things might actually be made from – which is only a problem if you are working in a studio surrounded by materials of one kind or another, and with some space to fill in an as yet unspecified and perhaps entirely imaginary gallery. Which is another way of saying that in art ideas are often much tidier creatures than objects. And then, to cut a rather long and very dull story short, at some point in the early 1990s my monochromes tripped up on a couple of readymades and stumbled into some colour. And in the process they began, just possibly, to have a life of their own, rather than one I had dreamed up for them.

In 1997 I also began taking photographs of what I called "found monochromes" in the streets around where I lived in London. My initial thought was that I would somehow refute a thesis I had recently heard being made by Jeff Wall in a lecture on the work of On Kawara. Wall had presented a rather vivid account of the history of modernism as the history of two opposed forces unable fully to escape each other and equally unable to be reconciled with one another. These forces were embodied in the painting of modern life, on the one hand, and high abstraction on the other, and they had found form in photojournalism and the monochrome, respectively. As I understood it, he appeared to be saying that, in its logic of exclusion and emptying out, the monochrome was in some structural way unable to engage with or embody the experience of modernity. That seemed a very plausible argument – except I just didn't buy it. So I went out into the street, literally, with the aim of finding evidence that the city is actually full of monochromes, that modernity is a precondition of the monochrome and that, in all its artificiality, the city is the monochrome's natural habitat, an unacknowledged museum of the inadvertent monochrome. None of which, I now realise, necessarily refuted Wall's thesis, but never mind.

On 17 November 1997 I photographed a monochrome I found on a street in King's Cross, near where I lived at the time. It was off-white and cracked, but I thought it would do the job if I could find another four or five to go with it. But then, slowly, or maybe not so slowly, something happened. I found there was something strange and rather compelling about these readymade blanks. And from time to time I found new ones. So I photographed them too. And in the process I learned a few things: a found monochrome has to be a blank surface in the street, but not just any blank surface. It has to be rectangular or square, vertical, white and in some sense inadvertent, unplanned, or temporary. For it to work, the monochrome has somehow to detach itself from its surroundings. That's why white is better than black or other colours (I photographed some reds and blues and yellows too, early on). And in detaching itself from the surroundings, by being white and parallel to the picture plane, the monochrome plane can begin to form a small empty centre in an otherwise saturated visual field. A bit of nothing – but more nothing-much than nothing-ness; a presence that is more like an absence, at least for a moment or two. Or, to put it another way, the monochrome became more interesting – more ambiguous, more uncertain – than I had been prepared for it to be. Rather than just a dumb blank or just a bit of exotic emptiness, it appeared that it might occasionally be both, or it might somehow flicker between the two mutually exclusive alternatives. A plane and a void. But not a mysterious void-in-general, rather a contingent void, a void in a place, here, today, on this particular railing in this particular street; here today, and probably gone tomorrow. A void in a place, but not in every place: these incidents are not, I noticed, distributed evenly throughout the city; they have a tendency to cluster in more overlooked and transitional environments, and are scarce in more refined and elegant districts. For me, and perhaps only for me, these bits of peripheral vision are little heroic moments, small monuments to modernity – if modernity can still, in part, be defined in that great phrase of Baudelaire's as "the ephemeral, the fugitive and the contingent".

Since 1997 I have found versions of these occasional void-planes in areas of London and in just about every other city I have travelled to. There were around 400 at the last count. I have come to think of the series as an open-ended project that changes shape as it grows and can be exhibited in a number of forms – as a slide show, as individual prints, as an installation of images pasted on a wall in a grid. Together the series forms a map of sorts: a city map; an autobiographical map; a mildly psycho-geographical map; and a map that principally indicates the location of something that is no longer there.

David Batchelor is an artist who lives and works in London. His work features in 'Colour Chart', Tate Liverpool.

Colour Chart III: How *Random Distribution of 40,000 Squares using the odd and Even Numbers of a Telephone Directory* (1960) came into being

François Morellet and **Ellsworth Kelly** in New York (1968), photographed by Danielle Morellet

65, 38, 21, 4, 72 …

BY FRANÇOIS MORELLET

The catalyst for the idea of the painting *Random Distribution of 40,000 Squares using the odd and Even Numbers of a Telephone Directory* (1960) came about after a conversation with Ellsworth Kelly, who at the time was living in France. He had recently visited Jean Arp's studio and talked about one of Arp and Sophie Taeuber's joint collages, *Squares Arranged to the Laws of Chance*, made in 1917. From an early stage in my career I looked for ways to take the fewest possible subjective decisions in the process of the creation of a painting. I wanted to be radically different from the lyrical abstraction of the École de Paris, which was the mainstream trend at that time, represented by popular artists such as Mathieu.

An earlier influence on how I thought about my painting came from a stay in Brazil, where my wife and I planned to emigrate to escape a possible third world war that threatened to spread from Korea during the early 1950s. In 1950 Max Bill had a big exhibition at the Museu de Arte Moderna in São Paulo, which had a tremendous impact. His work and approach (what he called "Concrete art") was a major influence in South America from that time and until now. I went over to Brazil shortly after this show, which I discovered only through photographs and enthusiastic comments from young Brazilian artists.

However, the legacy starting with Mondrian, followed by the Concrete movement with Theo van Doesburg, then with Bill, was preceded by my very first enthusiasm for Oceanian "Tapas" with their repetition of printed shapes, which I discovered at the ethnological Musée de l'Homme

of Paris in the 1940s. My third major shock came from the abstract Islamic networks of lines and repetitive pattern all over the walls of the Alhambra Palace in Granada on my first visit in 1952.

With *Random Distribution*, the purpose of my system was to cause a reaction between two colours of equal intensity. I drew horizontal and vertical lines to make 40,000 squares. Then my wife or my sons would read out the numbers from the phone book (except the first repetitive digits), and I would mark each square for an even number while leaving the odd ones blank. The crossed squares were painted blue and the blank ones red. For the 1963 Paris Biennale I made a 3-D version of it that was shown among the Groupe de Recherche d'Art Visuel installations (and re-created it again on different occasions). I wanted to create a dazzling fight between two colours that shared the same luminosity. This balance of colour intensity was hard to adjust because daylight enhances the blue and artificial light boosts the red. I wanted the visitors to have a disturbing experience when they walked into this room – to almost hurt their eyes with the pulsating, flickering balance of two colours. I like that kind of aggression.

François Morellet is an artist who lives and works in Cholet, France. Random Distribution of 40,000 Squares using the odd and Even Numbers of a Telephone Directory *is included in* 'Colour Chart' *at Tate Liverpool. His exhibition at the Museum Ritter, Waldenbuch, Germany, runs from 16 May to 26 September. A permanent site-specific piece,* L'Esprit d'escalier, *will be installed at the Musée du Louvre, Paris, later this year.*

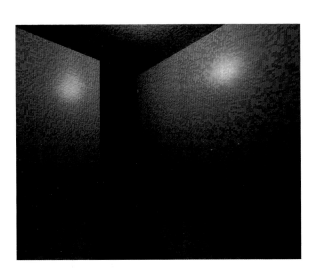

Installation view of
François Morellet's
Random Distribution at
Kunsthaus, Zurich (2006)
Wallpaper, carpet,
lightbulb, 460×430 cm

François Morellet
*Random Distribution of
40,000 Squares using the
odd and Even Numbers of a
Telephone Directory* (1960)
Oil on canvas
103×103 cm

'65, 38, 21, 4, 72...'

ARTIST ROOMS: Last year one of the largest donations of art in Britain was made by Anthony d'Offay. The collection of more than 700 works by leading artists, known as ARTIST ROOMS and assembled over the past 28 years, is now owned jointly by the National Galleries of Scotland (NGS) and Tate on behalf of the nation. This year Tate sites, NGS and thirteen museums and galleries across the UK are showing more than 30 ARTIST ROOMS in the first tour of the collection. TATE ETC. talks to Anthony D'Offay about the impetus behind the project, and also to a selection of the artists on display

ME, YOU, US

Poster for the **Andy Warhol** and **Joseph Beuys** exhibition at Galleria Lucio Amelio, Naples (1980)

ARTIST ROOMS: Tate and National Galleries of Scotland. Acquired jointly through The d'Offay Donation with assistance from the National Heritage Memorial Fund and The Art Fund 2008. Courtesy teknemedia. Photograph: Mimmo Jodice

BY ANTHONY D'OFFAY, GILDA WILLIAMS, GERHARD RICHTER, BILL VIOLA, VIJA CELMINS, ALEX KATZ & ED RUSCHA

Anthony d'Offay on Anthony d'Offay

Many years ago, in 1973, when we sold Jacob Epstein's marble sculpture *Doves* (1914) to Tate, I was looking at it with Richard Morphet, who was the deputy keeper of the modern collection. He said to me: "It's so wonderful; now it belongs to all of us." I thought that was a beautiful thing to say. So I hope that when the Diane Arbus room is showing at the National Museum Wales, or Bruce Nauman in Glasgow, Gerhard Richter in Middlesbrough or Robert Mapplethorpe in Inverness that the rooms will have the feeling of belonging to everyone in these places. I very much hope that ARTIST ROOMS will revolutionise the way galleries can show contemporary artists' work in this country. There is so little money that comes from central or local government for acquisitions, particularly to regional museums. ARTIST ROOMS is addressing that concern, and now if a gallery wants a room of Gilbert & George, Andy Warhol or Joseph Beuys, then it can have one tailored to its needs.

I think it is very important to get children to engage with art from an early age. My own defining experience was in the local museum in Leicester when I was eight. My mother would leave me there while she did the shopping. I remember that it had beautiful Egyptian antiquities, fantastic stuffed animals, birds' eggs, eighteenth-century porcelain and paintings and some extraordinary modern German paintings. There was also a great Lowry painting and a Francis Bacon. I was very inspired by the idea that you could be a living artist and show your work in the museum. After these visits I would go home and make little sculptures that looked like Egyptian mummies. You can have an acquaintance with works of art which then turns into a friendship, which turns into a love affair. It becomes part of your life, and that changes people, doesn't it? It becomes truth, a reality, and something on which you can lean hard and believe in throughout your life.

Anthony d'Offay on Joseph Beuys

In 1977 Anne Seymour and I got married. She had been for several years the curator of contemporary art at Tate. She had this laudable idea that I needed to be "reformed" (at that time I was involved in a lot of historical British shows) and said to me: "If you like, there is another adventure with contemporary art." So we felt there was an opportunity in London for a big international gallery where we could exhibit the great artists of the world, many of whom had not been shown in the city before. Beuys was the first on our list. I got the chance to meet him after the publishers Thames & Hudson asked me to take the proof copy of his

Guggenheim catalogue to his studio in Düsseldorf. The studio itself, which no longer exists, was just like one of his works – the floor was made of stitched leather.

We asked him if he would like to do the opening exhibition in our space and he agreed. In 1980 he came to London and made an installation called *Stripes from the House of the Shaman*, which is now in the National Gallery of Australia, in Canberra.

Beuys came from a different place than other artists. It wasn't an art background. He was coming from the fields of science and politics as well as ecological concerns. There was a quality of his work that asked a lot of questions, and that made you think about it. It was endlessly fascinating to sit and talk with him. He had this incredibly attractive side to him of being powerful and modest at the same time. When he came to London, often there would be other people that would come to the gallery – David Sylvester, Nicholas Serota, Richard Hamilton and Rita Donagh, Gilbert & George – who would bring out the best in him. Over time we felt very close to him and he made everything feel like an intellectual conversation in the family.

Anthony d'Offay on Andy Warhol

It sounds funny, but when I would visit Warhol in the early 1980s his reputation had fallen. People didn't like the late work, and there was a lot of feeling that he had become little more than a society portrait painter. I wanted very much to do a show with him, and asked him what he would like to do, but he would always say: "It's up to you. What would you like to do?" So I felt an obligation to think of something that worked from a critical point of view. Finally, I came up with the idea of an exhibition of self-portraits, which he loved, and the works in the show, which became known as the "Fright-Wigs", were an enormous critical success.

He was very easy to work with, but the surprising thing was that he was extremely shy. He had this shield up much of the time. You expected that he would be expansive and relaxed, but that only emerged when he was, say, taking a Polaroid of someone for a portrait. I think this apparently passive kind of approach allowed him to feel the essence of the world in which he lived, and to capture the important aspects of it that would resonate with the people who were living through it and stand the test of time. And it is true. If you look at Warhol's late pictures now, they look super-great. I can't think of many artists from the late 1970s and early 1980s whose work survives in that way. They still feel completely "of now", completely present, as if they are outside time.

Gilda Williams on Warhol's early drawings

We can not underestimate the intensive training Warhol received during ten solid, workaholic years as New York's best-known commercial illustrator. He spent more than a decade honing to perfection his natural genius for creating hugely communicative images which satisfied his elite consumers – a skill he later transferred with outrageous success to a fine art career. In these early drawings – with their pompadour hairstyles, dainty cherubs and rococo picture frames – we see a typical 1950s American still pursuing some European idea of sophistication. The news hadn't quite sunk in that America had won the culture wars too – with Warhol eventually emerging among the greatest victors.

The drawings can be dismissed as "not very interesting", as artist Mike Kelley recently has. Or we can read heavily into them for introducing the hallmarks of his mature practice: the impersonal blotting technique prefiguring the mechanised silkscreen; the lines of repeated butterflies and musical notes leading to the endless rows of Coke bottles and Marilyns. But the Warhol story is not just about art; it's a spectacular tale of self-transformation. When Truman Capote met Warhol during the time of these drawings, the author pitied him as a "born loser" – a most ironic epitaph for a man who achieved every form of public success possible: intellectual, financial, institutional, social, creative. From "colossal creep" (as Warhol was described in the early 1960s by New York socialite Frederick Eberstadt) he became, by 1965, just about the coolest man on earth. The drawings signal the pre-cool Andy, the Euro-wannabe in a bow tie and suit – before he went Pop and switched to cowboy boots and dark glasses. The Warhol behind them still let his effeminacy and immigrant origins slip into the work. They are the Before to his After, but without them the After may never have happened.

Gilda Williams is an art critic and visiting lecturer at Gold-smiths College and Sotheby's Institute of Art, London.

Gerhard Richter on *Two Sculptures for a Room by Palermo* (1971)

I really liked the wall paintings Blinky Palermo did. He had simply painted a room in the classic colour ochre yellow, with a neat frame left unpainted – about a hand's width – top, bottom, left, right – colour fields. It was classical in the modern age back then – it had this wonderful slight whiff of tradition I liked very much, and then I said that what it needs are sculptures in a room like that. Yeah – do it! We made those ourselves. I made a plaster of Paris mask of his face, he helped me with mine, and I modelled the rest to fit: the head, the hair, the ears, the back of the head.

These two heads are permanently exhibited in Munich. Of course, the walls aren't there, but the Munich people painted the walls yellow, as a tribute to Palermo. It's the typical Munich ochre colour. It's been done "like the original". There isn't a sign saying: "This is a work of art by Palermo." The only things on display were my two sculptures. They were only united with the Palermo walls for one exhibition. It wasn't a condition that the sculptures had to be shown with the Palermo walls. Back then, after the exhibition, I took the sculptures back home with me. And later still I had them cast in bronze. All in all, there are three pairs. One pair made of plaster of Paris, two made of bronze. I never learned how to do that. There are many specialists who make bronze casts. I did it in plaster of Paris back then. There is some fun to be had from making models. I never took lessons in sculpting.

This extract was taken from Gerhard Richter: Text – Writings, Interviews and Letters 1961–2007 *by Gerhard Richter, edited by Dietmar Elger and Hans Ulrich Obrist, recently published by Thames & Hudson.*

Bill Viola on *Catherine's Room* (2001)

Catherine's Room is based on the predella – an historical form of multi-panel painting that runs along the frame at the bottom of an altarpiece. Traditionally, it contained a chronological narrative depicting the lives of Jesus or the saints. To our eyes it looks like a movie storyboard. I was inspired by seeing a reproduction of Andrea di Bartolo's predella *St Catherine of Siena Praying* (c.1393). I created a piece with five video LCD screen panels that describe a chronological sequence, and then expanded it to include the idea of an eternal cycle. *Catherine's Room* contains a series of images of a woman alone in a room engaged in various activities. There is a small window, outside of which the branches of a tree are visible. In the first panel she is starting her day, doing some yoga. In the second panel she is doing her daily chores. The third panel takes place late in the day when she is engaged in writing at her desk. By the fourth panel it is night, and she is solemnly lighting more than 100 candles, one by one. In the final panel we see her preparing for bed and then going to sleep. Throughout these events, outside the window we also see the tree passing through its cycle of the seasons, from blossoms to bare branches.

Catherine's Room is a work that places the individual within the cycles of time and nature – the eternal patterns of a day, a year, a life. I think this is a piece that everybody can relate to. I remember when we first showed it in the Anthony d'Offay Gallery in 2001, I overheard a little girl saying to her mum: "This is like a doll house!" She said she wanted to stay all day and keep watching it forever.

Bill Viola is an artist based in Long Beach, California.

Andy Warhol
*A Hand of
Bridge* (1953)
Pen and ink,
graphite and
dye on paper
58.4×35.6 cm

Andy Warhol
Male Torso
(1956)
Pen and ink
on paper
42.5×34.9 cm

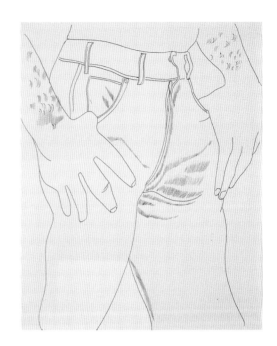

Installation view
of **Blinky Palermo**
and **Gerhard
Richter**'s *Wall
Painting and
Sculpture* (1971)
at Galerie
Heiner Friedrich,
Cologne

Bill Viola
*Catherine's
Room* (2001)
Video on five
LCD panel
displays
38.1×246×5.7cm

'Me, You, Us'

Vija Celmins
Concentric Bearings D
(1985)
Mezzotint,
aquatint,
drypoint and
photogravure
on paper
46×57cm

Alex Katz
City Night
(1998)
Oil on board
22.9×30cm

Vija Celmins

I'm an eastern European, so didn't see the desert until I moved to California in 1962. I would drive out into the desert. I liked it. It was a place that made you feel as if your body had no weight. At first I thought there was nothing there. Then I began to see things. I was always having to adjust my eyes back and forth – both far and close, which is how I think about my own work sometimes. It lies somewhere between distance and intimacy. That early discovery about that different kind of space – where you don't know really how far or near something is – had a subtle influence on my work, especially that of the late 1960s and 1970s.

After some five years of doing intense single images with no composition, but just subtle adjustments to the plane, I could stand it no longer, so I started putting one image next to another. Sort of just shoving them together… like a galaxy image that invites you in, next to a desert surface that projects out at you. It meant that when you were close to the work each eye would see a different image, or you would have to move your attention from one to the other, but when you pulled back a bit, the images seemed to be working together, and made for a more complex spatial experience. For a while I liked that, and I did a series of double and triple-image works using pictures, mostly torn from books and magazines, that I had collected over the years.

I'm creating a flat, invented world. Imagination comes in from building an image so that it has a physical reality with some real staying power. I try to make a work that is thoroughly considered and has a strong form. However, the manipulating of the surface is subtle and sensuous. It is in the nuances of the way the graphite feels and the marks that are left.

Vija Celmins is an artist based in New York.

Alex Katz

The sketch of the branches of the plane trees in *3pm November 1997* was done on the spot in the La Guardia Square gardens in New York just as the light was fading. *City Night* (1998) was also painted in New York. I remember that I painted that one just after I had eaten supper. When people see my paintings of nature they usually think they were done in Maine, or some other rural place – not central New York. It is unusual these days to paint *en plein air*, but I find it's the only way to get the information I need, and I don't want to rely on my memory. Painting in public is a bizarre experience as you can get mistaken for being an amateur painter. A few times I have had people come up to me and say something like: "I have a friend who owns a bar. He could exhibit some of your paintings."

I studied antique drawing and modern art. That was okay, but I knew that I wanted something more immediate. So when I first saw Jackson Pollock's paintings – bingo! I like painting direct from nature and doing it quickly. It's like a performance. The painting is both controlled and casual. The idea is to make the paint fluid and make a fluid surface. I try to be specific with the form not being constrained. So I see it as post-abstract painting, which I think separates me from other figurative painters. I am an image maker, I have a very "cool" technique, but my subject matter is pretty dull – I don't do crucifixions; I don't do sex.

I remember as a child my father telling me – why don't you paint your own backyard. (Usually artists were painting what came before them art historically.) I knew my father was right. Yet twenty or 30 years ago, people didn't get my work – they thought it was bad Pop Art or bad photo-realist painting. Now it is seen as very American – both here and abroad. And since Bice Curiger's group exhibition 'Birth of the Cool' in Zurich and the Saatchi Gallery's exhibition of my paintings in London (both in 1997), I got noticed in Europe. Now I'm treated like a dead person – because of the respect I get.

Alex Katz is an artist based in New York.

Ed Ruscha

TATE ETC. What is the origin of the texts in your works *Soapy Smith*, *Pretty Eyes, Electric Bills* and *Smells Like Back of Old Hot Radio*?

ED RUSCHA Soapy Smith was a con man who lived in Denver, Colorado, in the 1880s. He would incite crowds by saying: "Buy my soap and inside the wrapper might be a $20 bill." Many people found $20 bills, but they were all part of the scam. This made him temporarily wealthy. *Pretty Eyes, Electric Bills* is my way of separating two subjects that are on the far end of the world from each other. This somehow gets to be the reason that I want to make a work of art of this discord. And *Smells Like Back of Old Hot Radio* is based on a childhood experience: the aroma of a wooden-cased radio that has been turned on for an hour or so. It's the declaration of a simple smell – the hot tubes within the radio mixing with the oils in the wood. Takes me back.

TATE ETC. They are like poetic readymades. Does poetry come into your take on words?

ED RUSCHA I once thought poetic was a nerdy word, but finally I cannot think of another one to replace it. Poetry, as vague as it is, enters my work, as does geology, archeology, music, together with some of the most crass, mundane thoughts on the planet.

TATE ETC. Your art seems positive and assured. Is there any anxiety at work underneath it?

ED RUSCHA I am an anxious person, so pressures play a part in what I would call blind faith choices in my art. Whenever I can be empathic or deliberate, then I think I've gone down the right road.

TATE ETC. You once said: "I'm dead serious about being nonsensical." Is the humour intended to add a layer of meaning or distance?

ED RUSCHA I am not a big fan of meaning. Logic is also another nebulous thought. I attempt to bring threads of subjects, however shaggy, to my work and inject little suggesters to the picture itself, and this often puts a smile on my face.

Ed Ruscha is an artist based in Venice, California. His exhibition at the Hayward Gallery runs from 14 October to 10 January.

ARTIST ROOMS *was established through The Anthony d'Offay Donation in 2008, with the assistance of the National Heritage Memorial Fund, The Art Fund and the Scottish and British Governments.* ARTIST ROOMS *is shared with museums and galleries throughout the UK with thanks to the support of independent charity The Art Fund and, within Scotland, the Scottish Government.*

Ian Hamilton Finlay, Tate Britain, until 2010; Vija Celmins, Damien Hirst, Ellen Gallagher, Alex Katz, Andy Warhol, Francesca Woodman, Scottish National Gallery of Modern Art, Edinburgh, until 8 November; Andy Warhol, Wolverhampton Art Gallery, until 21 September; Anselm Kiefer, Jeff Koons, Jannis Kounellis, Ed Ruscha, Robert Therrien, Andy Warhol, Tate Modern, until 2010; Bruce Nauman, Tramway, Glasgow, until 31 May; Gilbert & George, Tate Britain, 2010; Robert Mapplethorpe, Inverness Museum and Art Gallery, until 27 June; Sol LeWitt, Tate Liverpool, 12 May – 13 September; Richard Long, Ulster Museum, National Museums Northern Ireland, 20 May – May 2010; Lawrence Weiner, Tate St Ives, 16 May – 20 September; Diane Arbus, National Museum Cardiff, 9 May – 19 August; Andy Warhol, New Art Gallery, Walsall, 15 May – 5 July; Bill Viola, Pier Arts Centre, Stromness, Orkney, 19 June – 5 September; Joseph Beuys, De la Warr Pavilion, Bexhill-on-Sea, 4 July – 27 September; Agnes Martin, Scottish National Gallery of Modern Art, Edinburgh, 6 August – 8 November; Gerhard Richter, Middlesbrough Institute of Modern Art, 28 August - 15 November; Ron Mueck, Aberdeen Art Gallery, 29 August – 31 October; Jenny Holzer, The Lightbox, Woking, 14 November – 14 February 2010; Robert Mapplethorpe, Graves Gallery, Museums Sheffield, 19 December – 27 March 2010, Johan Grimonprez, firstsite, Colchester (Offsite Project), opens in the autumn.

Ed Ruscha
Smells Like Back of Old Hot Radio (1976)
Pastel on paper
58.6×75.2cm

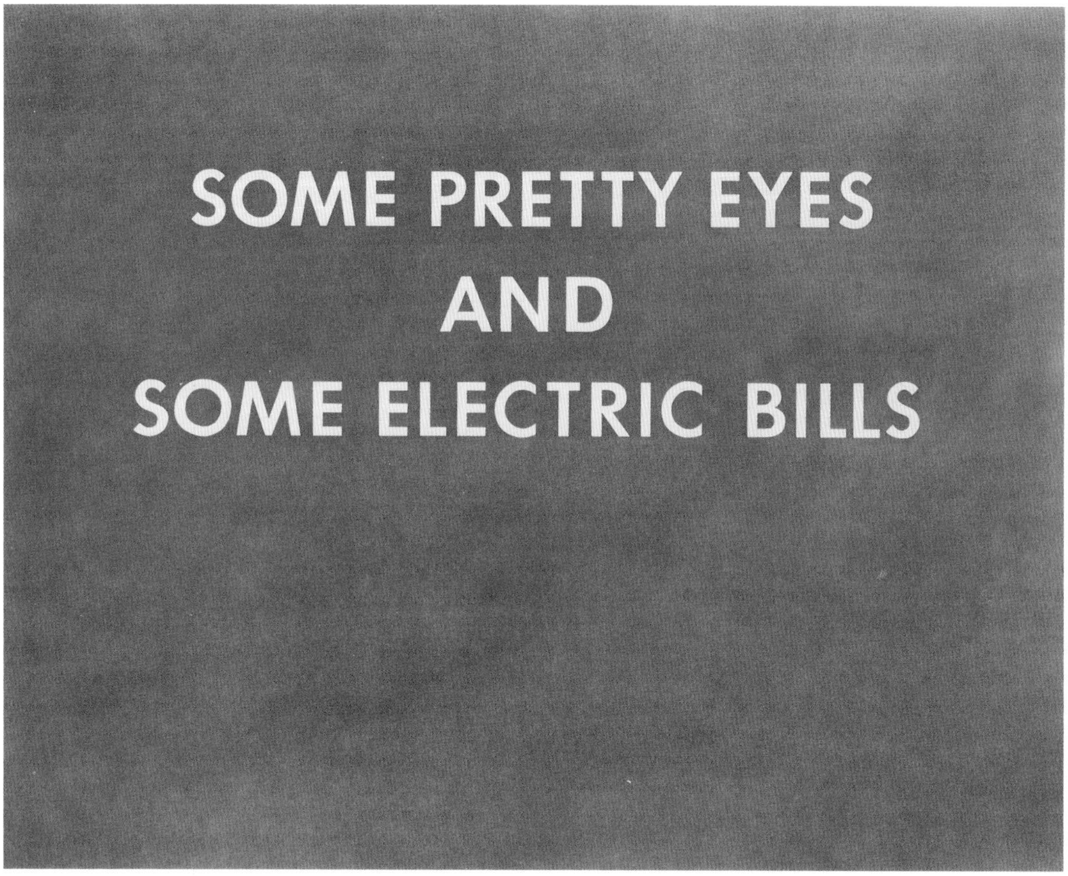

Ed Ruscha
Pretty Eyes,
Electric Bills
(1976)
Mixed media
on paper
57.4×72.1 cm

<u>Eva Rothschild:</u> For the latest Duveen Commission at Tate Britain, Eva Rothschild has created a startling new sculpture that will weave its way through the gallery's central space, reflecting her previous work's blending of contemporary interpretations of sculptural traditions with her distinctive voice

Installation view of **Eva Rothschild**'s exhibition at South London Gallery (2007). Left to right: *Garlands*, *The Rock and the Arch*, *The Inside of Your Head*, *Mr. Messy*, *Riches*, *Jokes*

A LEXICON OF FORMS

BY CAOIMHÍN MAC GIOLLA LÉITH

Eva Rothschild's sculptures have been likened to "artefacts from some lost civilisation or from some post-apocalyptic scenario" whose symbolic meanings have all but faded from memory or lie just beyond our current imaginings. Though leavened by wit and humour, especially evident in the choice of titles, their occasional intimations of esoteric magic also hint at something darker. Many perch on spindly stands, while some jut out from high corners, or arc precariously overhead, or appear to hover improbably in mid-air, a narrow cascade of coloured leather strips obscuring their support. Though fundamentally stable, they often appear to twist on their axes or teeter precariously.

Her lexicon of forms is instantly recognisable, but surprisingly varied. It includes thick lumpen masses, thin angular slabs, sinuous coils, woven sheets, shaggy fringes and, above all, slender rods of painted wood that kink crazily here and there, creating complex, off-kilter geometries in space. Her work is informed by the legacy of sculpture forged through processes of industrial production and, in common with that of a number of her peers, obliquely acknowledges the precedent of certain strains of 1960s sculpture, as well as more general aspects of 1960s counter-culture. Yet it has always seemed even more apparently indebted to the tradition of domestic or artisanal craftsmanship.

Despite an unerring command of the exhibition installation as a format, as seen in particular in her solo show at the South London Gallery in the winter of 2007, Rothschild has always insisted on her works as individual sculptures rather than elements in an installation. Her commission to produce a single sculpture for Tate Britain's Duveen galleries has, however, provided the opportunity to work on an unprecedented scale. Running the length of the galleries, this new site-responsive sculpture, still in development and so far untitled at the time of writing (her pieces are never untitled), is designed to occupy a large space and yet will have little volume. Made up of a series of frame-like structures, some of which run along the ground and others of which are elevated, it is envisaged by the artist as a kind of "temporary architecture", such that the engaged viewer navigating the space will sometimes feel as if he or she is "inside" the sculpture and sometimes "outside". While many of her previous sculptures have made comparable use of open volumes, this commission has provided the welcome challenge to brush against the grain of auratic self-containment characteristic of much of her work in recent years.

Faced with the potentially intimidating grandeur of Tate Britain's central axis, there is an obvious temptation to take command of the space by responding in kind with a comparably imposing work of considerable physical substance. Richard Serra's *Weight and Measure*, which occupied the galleries in 1992, is the most memorable precedent. Rothschild's decision to opt for lightness rather than heaviness is nevertheless emphatic in its own way, as well as being entirely in keeping with the nature of her art. As she says: "I knew from the start that I wanted something that didn't obscure the space, but that just tangled with your perception of it and travelled through it touching as lightly as possible on the architecture."

Colour has played an important role in Rothschild's sculptural vocabulary too. It has been crucial, for instance, to many works employing woven patterns of almost psychedelic discordance. It has also functioned as a means of teasing the eye into confusing the thin zigzagging lines of a piece constructed largely of slender wooden batons. She was quite sure, however, that in this case her sculpture's lines should be as clear as possible, hence the decision to limit herself to one colour – black. This decision is consistent with Rothschild's long-standing ambition to produce the kind of sculpture that can be perceived to be complete and whole in itself, while simultaneously constituting a source of productive confusion to the eye and mind alike.

Tate Britain Duveen Commission: Eva Rothschild, supported by Sotheby's, Tate Britain, 30 June – 29 November, curated by Katharine Stout, curator of contemporary British art.

Caoimhín Mac Giolla Léith is senior lecturer at the School of Irish Celtic Studies, University College, Dublin.

Eva Rothschild at South London Gallery (2007). Left to right: *Rising Sun*, *Higher Love*, *Cactus*

Per Kirkeby: To coincide with Tate Modern's exhibition of paintings by the Danish artist, the career of Per Kirkeby is explored – from his Pop motifs borrowed from Hergé's Tintin books to his monumental architectonic sculptures

POLYMATH OF OUR TIME

BY ROBERT STORR

A good deal of the art history being written today isn't art history at all. Rather, it consists of exercises in anachronistic classification in which artists are assigned tags and lined up in groups according to ideological and stylistic genealogies. The rubric of Conceptualism, for example, becomes the catch-all basket for a disparate array of aesthetic practices, notably textual art, appropriated and manipulated photos, the hard core performance art, video, installation art, readymade sculpture and allied sub-genres. When it comes to identifying the antithesis – if not nemesis – of Conceptualism for those who deem it the only true path for progressive postmodernists, the usual suspect is painting. It would appear equally obvious to such pro-pomos that painters have nothing much to do with Conceptualism, although licences to paint are issued to, among others, artists such as Art & Language, John Baldessari and Gerhard Richter, that one-man undoer of all dogmas.

Still, the art historical record seldom reflects many of the more intriguing anomalies buried with current customs of classification. Take the case of Per Kirkeby, and, for contrariness sake, begin at the beginning of this Danish artist's long career with a group of works that are usually ignored, and a few pertinent facts that are habitually glossed over when his name comes up. The paintings, few in number, are square mixed-media works on masonite dating from 1968 and 1969. Kirkeby was just entering his thirties at the time, having abandoned the university study of natural history he began in 1957 to enter the Experimental Art School in Copenhagen in 1962, a year after it was opened as an alternative to the Royal Academy. Already behind him was intensive work as an academic and field geologist – as Lasse B Antonsen writes in one of the best synoptic accounts of his early career, Kirkeby took part in two expeditions to Greenland in 1958 and 1962. Ahead of him at the Experimental School were life-altering encounters with recent and current vanguard art, notably that of the paintings of Wols, the drawings and poems of Henri Michaux, the music of John Cage, the multi-media events of Fluxus and the art and mentorship of Joseph Beuys (who Kirkeby first met when both showed up a day early for one of Beuys's actions at the Royal Academy). In short, Kirkeby was a polymath in tune with his times, which is to say a well-educated man and an improviser all at once.

Unsurprisingly, his early masonite paintings are a vigorous aggregate of multiple aesthetic precedents, with lots of raw, youthful ingenuity and energy thrown in. Within their equilateral formats the unstable colours and gestures of *informel* – more specifically those of the Cobra movement with its foothold in Copenhagen – bump up against the bright hues and hard-contoured shapes of British and American Pop, while spectres of late nineteenth and early twentieth-century Danish landscape painting grow in the cracks between the many-faceted modernism that prevails.

It is significant, given these artistic compass points, that the Pop element does not quote New York advertising, Hollywood movies or mainstream American comics, but instead lifts its motifs from Hergé's Tintin books, and imports the exoticism for which the Belgian cartoonist was loved by adolescents throughout Europe and is now condemned by post-colonial critics everywhere. It is easy to see how the adventurer in Kirkeby, the young geologist-turned-artist, would have been attracted to Hergé's crisp depictions of faraway places and fantastic events – in particular the stories of Tintin's excursion to the Himalayas, and the landing of a comet on a remote island. From

Per Kirkeby
standing on the
site of a work in
progress in Lund,
Sweden (1991)

these stories he borrowed the image of a Tibetan stupa (a Buddhist religious monument), a giant mushroom spurred to mutant proportions by the comet and other details. The end product is a kind of collage romanticism elaborated by brushy passages of pure painterly painting, loose silhouettes and a snappy, all-over agitation of the surface that recalls the early works of the Swedish polymath Öyvind Fahlström, of whom Kirkeby must have known, and graphic dreaminess of the American recluse Jess, about whom he could not have known.

Why dwell on these paintings and their moment? In order to adjust our perspective sufficiently to encompass Kirkeby's whimsy and the breadth of his knowledge about cutting-edge art of that febrile era. And why is that necessary now, on the occasion of his retrospective at Tate Modern? Because he has become a captive of categories in which he does not completely fit, as a consequence of the streamlining of history, and because even his defenders have stressed his links to northern European nature painting to the point that his particular reasons for painting nature, and his peculiar ways of denaturing painting, tend to get lost. Between the old-time religionists of 1980s Neo-Expressionism and the stern iconoclasm of Neo-Expressionism enemies, Kirkeby has too frequently been typecast when he has been given any prominent role in the story of post-war art. In that respect, the early Tintin paintings are a useful touchstone, as they hint at the wide range of his interests and activities. Yet, while full of seemingly incommensurable images and effects, they do not explain themselves. Already they display the strange mixture of alternating pictorial transparency and opacity and momentary flashes of pure poetry that henceforth distinguish his paintings.

If northern light is to be taken as the hallmark of Scandinavian art, then Kirkeby is among the handful of Scandinavian artists who, although he himself rarely paints landscape as such, have captured that light in all hours of the day (such as those sudden changes in weather that can turn a radiant sky into a dense wall of clouds and back again). Presently, there seems to be little enthusiasm among people with advanced taste or ideas for such naturalism, even when translated into abstract terms as Kirkeby does. This, and the fact that he didn't use painting to undertake a re-examination of history's horrors as Anselm Kiefer, Jörg Immendorff, Richter and his German contemporaries did – being Danish spared him the daylight nightmares they suffered – leaves him odd man out of the group of painters that claimed the stage at the beginning the 1980s. Perhaps a "greening" of art will change things and put him back in the mix thematically. In any event, he holds his own simply as a painter, and ultimately it is the freshness of his work in that medium upon which his reputation will primarily – and securely – rest.

The other foundation upon which Kirkeby's reputation sits is sculpture, specifically monumental, architectonic sculptures. Some of these monuments are made of clay or cast in bronze and are no bigger than the palm of one's

Per Kirkeby and
Bjørn Nørgaard with
Jörg Immendorff's
Fotonegerchen,
Aachen, Germany
(1967)

Per Kirkeby
*The Murder in Finnerup
Barn* (1967)
Mixed media on masonite
122 × 122 cm

Per Kirkeby
Nikopeja II (1996)
Oil on canvas
200×200 cm

Per Kirkeby
Brett – Felsen (2000)
Oil on canvas
220×200 cm

hand. Others built of brick would be big enough to house a family were it not that they are either open to the elements or entirely sealed off like tombs. These constructions are symbolically and stylistically polyvalent and, as such, ambiguous if not deliberately mysterious. Quite a few are reminiscent of Romanesque sanctuaries, except that Kirkeby avoids the kitschiness of readymade ruins familiar to us from seventeenth, eighteenth and nineteenth-century follies. Others have a decided modern aspect as if they were incomplete Danish buildings, and a couple enter into indirect dialogue with Sol LeWitt's cinder-block sculptures – on account of their masonry-based modularity and their allusions to monumental forms that come down to us from antiquity.

To speak of these as outdoor sculptures or monuments can be misleading on two counts. First, they commemorate nothing. Kirkeby is not a symbolist in that sense, much less a socially or ceremonially minded one. Second, they are not there just to be looked at, or at least not by a static spectator. Rather, the artist intends that they be walked around and, in some cases, through, so that one simultaneously experiences them visually and kinetically, effectively remaking them as a physical, spatial and mental gestalt from multiple viewpoints. To that extent they are closer to installation art than to sculpture as it is conventionally thought of, albeit a kind of installation art in which obdurate permanence is among the most powerful attributes. The other attribute is not contained in the material substance of the work itself, but expressed in its capacity to annex and frame its immediate environment. In most instances, nature is a primary component of what surrounds the sculptures, although such natural phenomena are already domesticated – no false wilderness mars Kirkeby's settings with melodrama – and the parks where his monuments are located along with the ambient buildings always remind one of an immanent urban reality. For Kirkeby, nature and culture are never antagonists, but always collaborators. That is true of his art generally.

In an age when simple contraction was the starting point and heightened contradiction the end point of so much work, Kirkeby has focused if not on synthesis, then on balancing different media in a mutually enhancing tension. The results, which entail coming back to aspects of modern art that post-modernity thought had been left behind forever, but which actual re-engagement shows are still vital, are grounding. And in Kirkeby's moody, thoughtful way, they are affirmative.

'Per Kirkeby', supported by the Per Kirkeby Supporters Group, the Danish Arts Agency and Stanley Thomas Johnson Foundation, Tate Modern, 17 June–6 September, curated by Achim Borchardt-Hume and assistant curator Cliff Lauson.

Robert Storr is an artist, critic and curator, and dean of the Yale School of Art.

FORGET ME NOT

BY GEOFF DYER

I'm not entirely sure that this is the picture I am writing about. Three or four years ago… And here we have another problem. It *feels* like three or four years ago, but time passes at such a rate that, in recent years, there have been quite a few instances when I'd thought something had taken place a couple of years ago only to discover that it actually occurred in the previous century. So it's possible that by "three or four years" I mean eight or nine.

Anyway, at some point in the last decade I was killing time – however quickly it passes, there are always odd pockets that need somehow to be disposed of – at Tate Britain, cruising the Turners. His output was so huge that you are always coming across pictures you've never seen before. On this occasion the painting that took my eye showed – as I remember it – figures in some kind of room or cellar, confronted by a source of intense and radiant light.

Although I can't remember when it happened or exactly what the painting looked like, I remember, very clearly, the jolt of seeing it for the first time. I took some notes that I've been unable to locate and which I never got round to writing up properly. I probably intended using the painting in a piece of fiction, contriving a situation in which someone encountered it in a gallery or in reproduction, or found themselves in a real-life equivalent of the scene depicted.

What kind of scene might this have been? In the late 1990s I spent quite a few nights at underground parties in venues whose settings – the cavernous railway arches near London Bridge, for example – closely resembled the architecture in the painting. Typically, there'd be a warren of rooms, the exact layout of which could never quite be committed to memory. You wandered from room to room, each promising – courtesy of the light and sound emanating from it – something alluring and magical. Often the lights made the other party-goers seem non-corporeal, spectral.

Outside every set of arches you stood on the threshold of beckoning revelation. A revelation akin to the one that Turner's painting simultaneously promises – and refuses – to reveal.

Since we are talking here about memory, I wonder if these words – room, threshold, revelation – immediately suggest to you another cultural artefact…

Yes, exactly, Andrei Tarkovsky's *Stalker*. Having guided the Professor and the Writer through the Zone, the Stalker brings them to the threshold of the Room where their deepest wishes will come true. On the brink of being granted this defining illumination they falter and turn back. In place of revelation there is uncertainty, doubt.

It has often been observed that the desolate beauty of Tarkovsky's Zone imaginatively prefigures the 30-kilometre exclusion zone surrounding Chernobyl, at the heart of which the damaged reactor was sealed in the so-called sarcophagus. (Many of Robert Polidori's Chernobyl photographs in his 2003 book, *Zones of Exclusion*, could double as stills from the set of Tarkovsky's film.)

The source of recessed light in Turner's painting does not look natural – especially since everything about the interior suggests that it is a cellar, some kind of subterranean dungeon. It is an emanation of pure energy. It is the annihilating light that the artist, according to D H Lawrence, "always sought": a light that would "transfuse the body, till the body was carried away, a mere bloodstain". It is the light of definitive or clinching revelation, which, for Lawrence, represents Turner's ultimate vision and ambition: "A white incandescent surface, the same whiteness when he finished as when he began, proceeding from nullity to nullity, through all the range of colour."

The picture I remembered seeing was like a representation of Turner moving – or, better, *being drawn* – towards this beckoning but unachievable vision. It gives visual expression to the same longing for transcendence articulated by Shelley (in 1821, in *Adonais*) as "the white radiance of Eternity".

This is not the only way in which the painting seems to be an essay on itself and the way it is perceived.

Our memories of works of art have an existence that is independent of, but contingent on, the works themselves. The ratio of independence to contingency is perhaps determined not just by us – by the vagaries and deficiencies of memory – but by the art itself. So it is no accident that this painting has failed to imprint itself on my memory with the precision and tenacity of a Canaletto, say, or a Holbein.

The walls – assuming that the picture reproduced here *is* the one I saw back whenever it was – are insubstantial. The figures are insubstantial. Nothing is as substantial as that core of molten light. Everything else, all that is solid, looks like it could melt into air. The interior depicted has been painted over a view of a landscape, so that it resembles a murky X-ray of how it came into being. The painting is a palimpsest, seemingly containing traces or memories of its own earlier existence. And it's obviously unfinished, suspended in the process of becoming what it is. The location and setting are neither given nor ascertainable. The title, *Figures in a Building* (Turner's or cataloguer's shorthand?), could hardly be less specific. The exact date of composition (circa 1830–1835) is unknown. According to Tate's online catalogue, it is "one of several works where Turner seems to be developing a historical subject without any very clear direction, as if hoping a theme might occur as he moved his paints around on the canvas". Even the artist, in other words, did not know what the picture might be about, working on it in the hope of a revelation that was never achieved.

Given all of this, it is hardly surprising that I couldn't remember the painting clearly – it's *inevitable*. Isn't that exactly what the picture *is* about, the way that some experiences – of art and life – remain unassimilable? (And, while we're at it, unphotographable: almost everything that makes the painting interesting is lost in the version you are seeing.) For all its haziness, the painting is a precise and lucid depiction of two refusals (both of which have their equivalents in Tarkovsky's film). First, of the world's inexhaustible refusal to succumb to the means of representation (if it did, we would be faced not with the end of history but the end of art). Second, the refusal of certain artworks to be reduced to memory. That, I think, is what makes the painting unforgettable.

Figures in a Building is no longer on display at Tate Britain. It is back in the vaults where, presumably, it blazes away like the light emerging within it.

JMW Turner's Figures in a Building *(c.1830–1835) was accepted by the nation as part of the Turner Bequest in 1856.*

Geoff Dyer's last book, The Ongoing Moment, *won the Infinity Award from the International Center of Photography. His new novel,* Jeff in Venice, Death in Varanasi, *is published by Canongate.*

JMW Turner
Figures in a Building
(c.1830-1835)
Oil on canvas
131×162cm

IMAGE / WORD

John Cage famously said that musicians in the post-war world had to learn from visual artists, while poet Frank O'Hara called himself the *balayeur des artistes*, or sweeper-up after artists. What is it that fascinates artists about those in other fields, drawing them across the lines, to listen, to watch and sometimes to engage in the cross-pollination of working together? Artists see something of themselves and something different in these other artists; they realise there is a unique opportunity there for expansion.

Sometimes groups of artists in different fields gather together to live and work. Particular constellations that compel us by their hybridity can clarify aspects of the individual artists' personalities and needs. Interactions can take the form of collaborations, published criticism, attempts to promote one another's work, or simply learning from conversation and example. The modern idea of hybridity goes back at least as far as Baudelaire, who was a classic example of the poet-critic. Since his time, his has been a standard to live up to.

In fact, this has been a tradition that has its roots in Paris. Apollinaire, Picasso and Gertrude Stein were at the centre of a group that became immortal as much for its interactions – including an alleged theft of the *Mona Lisa* from the Louvre, for which Apollinaire and Picasso were briefly arrested – as for each artist's towering individual achievements. The French tradition included theatre pieces, such as *Parade*, a joint venture by Picasso, Cocteau, Satie, Massine and Diaghilev, as well as many collaborative books and films. For the Surrealists, crossing over aesthetically was an embodiment of their belief in crossing over psychologically – both involve relinquishing conscious control.

The School of Paris gave way to the New York School, and while the first generation New York painters were not known for collaborations, they were hugely influential and set the tone for other artists, as Cage noted. The New York School poets pursued an informality in their compositions influenced by the Abstract Expressionist painters; they were equally informed by French writers and in some ways can be seen as an offshoot of the French tradition. The Baudelairean poet-critic returned in the poets Frank O'Hara, John Ashbery and James Schuyler, and collaboration was a life-blood for their friend Kenneth Koch, artists Jim Dine, Alex Katz, Larry Rivers and others.

In five lesser-known examples that I include here, we can see that encounters between poetry and the visual arts are, if not the rule, then definitely not the exception. Through their work we may get hints of what brought these artists together in the first place. I have been able to detect the following arc: classic modernists drew on each other's energies to reinforce their own monolithic ambitions; post-war artists were much more eclectic in choices of friends, styles and media; artists working today seem to have retreated to the relatively safe domain of the book, though imbuing it with relentlessly experimental fantasy.

In the years leading up to the First World War, Blaise Cendrars had the idea of writing a big poem, and he succeeded, with *La Prose du Transsibérien et de la petite Jehanne de France*. Similar to Apollinaire's Cubist poems, in which punctuation is jettisoned and ideas allowed to flow backwards and forwards ambiguously in their syntactical settings, *La Prose* is a *tour de force* of energetic motion – the train ride from Europe to Asia, with its wilful disruptions of time and place, forging a powerful metaphor for the artist's desire to be free from bourgeois limitations. With its contemporary language and images and freedom from literary reference, Cendrars's poetry, it can be argued, is even more modern than Apollinaire's. He believed *La Prose* would find its appropriate home in a visual setting, and therefore contacted Sonia Delaunay, a Russian émigré living in Paris, whose work had an appropriate openness. Delaunay later recalled her reaction to the poet's idea: "I proposed that we create a book that, unfolded, would be two metres high. I sought inspiration in the text for colour harmonies that would parallel the poem's unfolding. We chose characters of different fonts and sizes, a revolutionary procedure at the time." Together they produced the printed edition of the poem with Delaunay's *pochoir* counterpart. The publishers (*Les Hommes nouveaux*, a journal and press founded by Cendrars and Emile Szytta) called it the first *livre simultané*, meaning one saw the whole thing at a glance, like a painting or billboard, a comparison Cendrars himself underscored. *La Prose* was published in 1913 and had the desired result. Presented in Paris, Berlin, London, New York, Moscow and St Petersburg, it brought Cendrars the acclaim he desired. As the critic Marjorie Perloff notes: "It became not only a poem but an event, a happening."

Jean Cocteau in a birdcage at his *Spectacle Forain* in Paris (1961)

BY VINCENT KATZ

Henri Gaudier-Brzeska carving *Hieratic Head of Ezra Pound* (c.1914), photographed by Walter Benington

Howard Kanovitz, Kyle Morris, Larry Rivers, Donald Sanders and Kenneth Koch (in plane) prepare for Koch's play *The Red Robins* at the Guild Hall's John Drew Theatre in Southampton, New York (1977)

'Image / Word'

Detail of **Blaise
Cendrars** and **Sonia
Delaunay**'s *La Prose
du Transsibérien et
de la petite Jehanne
de France* (1913)
Four sheets, each
54×38cm

Joe Brainard and
Frank O'Hara
*Is That the Height
of Your Ambition
Johnny?* (1964)
Collage and ink
on paper
25.7×20.6cm

Blaise Cendrars
and **Fernand
Léger**'s
illustrated pages
from *La Fin du
monde filmee par
l'ange N.D* (1919)
Four sheets, each
33×25.5cm

The choices artists make are revealing. Why did Pound in 1908, at the age of 23, move from the US to London? He had a masters degree in romance philology and had been teaching at Wabash College in Indiana. Dead broke, he barely supported himself as a writer. Clearly, he had a strong desire to be around other artists, and visual artists played an important role in shaping his aesthetic. Pound may have seen in the visual arts a more public level of success than that achieved by most poets. Like Cendrars, he wanted to become more visible. In London, he met artists he thought were world-class, and enlisted them in his quest to create history. The energy of the Italian Futurists exerted great influence on Pound and his new cohorts, painter Wyndham Lewis and sculptor Henri Gaudier-Brzeska. A movement would be helpful. Trying to get away from Symbolism, which Pound found too flowery, not concrete enough, he helped to form the Imagist literary movement, beginning in 1912. Like Cendrars and Delaunay, he wanted images that could be perceived at a glance. As he wrote: "'Image' is that which presents an intellectual and emotional complex in an instant of time." In 1913, a year after the first Futurist exhibition in London, Pound coined the term Vorticism for the work Wyndham Lewis was making – and later organised Vorticist exhibitions in London (1915) and New York (1917). The vehicle would be Lewis's journal *Blast*, which Pound helped to edit. The First World War interrupted *Blast*'s publication, but Pound continued his active role. Reading his and Lewis's letters to one another, one can follow Pound's efforts to sell Lewis's works to the American collector John Quinn and to get Lewis's novel *Tarr* published. Their correspondence is frequent, business-like and also intimate, dealing as much with the reception of their aesthetic stances as with prospects for publication or sales.

Gaudier-Brzeska was a dynamic figure in Pound's circle, writing a Vorticist manifesto and producing an exuberant body of sculpture and drawing. His most ambitious work is the *Hieratic Head of Ezra Pound* (1914), made from a piece of marble Pound procured for him, in which the simplified shapes of the poet's brow and features hark back to earlier depictions of gods. The influence and desire work both ways: the poet emulated artists, and the artists were inspired by the poet. After Gaudier-Brzeska was killed in action in 1915, Pound not only acted as his executor, but also composed a memoir of his friend.

Pound's influence was enormous, and three young poets in São Paulo, Brazil, in the early 1950s, took his example in a particular direction: they became the inventors of Concrete Poetry. One of Pound's discoveries had been his interpretation of the Chinese ideogram as a vehicle capable of instant poetic expression. Another was his division of poetry into *logopoeia*, *melopoeia* and *phanopoeia*, roughly translatable as sense, music and image. Augusto de Campos, Haroldo de Campos and Décio Pignatari took these cues, creating a body of work that continues to

resonate today in the practice of many Brazilian and American poets. The name they gave to what they did – Concrete Poetry – was adopted in Europe and the United States as a term that could encompass work by both poets and visual artists that had a condensed literary and visual impact. Significantly, they were in contact with contemporary Brazilian artists, such as Hélio Oiticica, who were experimenting with similar ideas. Augusto de Campos has spoken of his work as a poetry of refusals, of limitations, similar to the limitations placed on their art by Brazilian Concrete artists of the 1950s. First published in 1958 in the journal *Noigandres*, the "Pilot Plan For Concrete Poetry" makes the following claims: "Concrete poetry takes account of graphic space as a structural agent… in the visual arts (spatial by definition) time intervenes (Mondrian and his *Boogie Woogie* series, Max Bill, Albers and perceptive ambiguity, concrete art in general)." Interestingly, they conclude by calling their work "absolute realism", in contrast to an art of expression. The form should ideally be identical to the content.

Augusto de Campos went on to produce "Popcrete Poems", as he calls them, in which no words at all are used, but the images are so strictly chosen and sequenced that they function like letters or words, or, in fact, like modern ideograms. In other visual poems, he thickly layers text, sometimes in closely related colours, making it difficult to decipher the meanings. The Brazilian Concrete poets reflect a decidedly urban experience. Like Cendrars and Delaunay and the Imagist Pound, they often create works that can be seen at a glance and have the communicative power of billboards.

Augusto de Campos's Popcrete poem *Eye for Eye* (1964) Collage on paper

Most of the time, when poets and visual artists are able to be in close proximity, it is because they have chosen to live in urban centres. Sometimes they find more rural settings in which to meet. Black Mountain College in North Carolina became one such centre from the 1930s through the 1950s. The experimental institution made the arts central to the teaching; there were collaborative theatre performances, including the first "happening", led by Cage and Merce Cunningham. There was also an emphasis on book publication and joint projects involving artists and poets. The poet Charles Olson, Black Mountain's last rector, forced poets to look at visual art and artists to read poetry. Cy Twombly, who studied at Black Mountain, asked Olson to write a preface for an exhibition he had in 1952. Olson recognised Twombly's emerging talent; he grappled with the work, final blurting: "The dug up stone figures, the thrown down glyphs, the old sorrels in sheep dirt in caves, the flaking iron – there are his *paintings*." Olson got poet Robert Creeley, then living in Majorca, to edit the *Black Mountain Review*, in which poets commented on artists' work. The magazine became highly influential in the poetry world, giving rise to the Black Mountain School of Poetry.

Through Pound, Creeley had met the French artist René Laubies, who first translated Pound into French. Creeley collaborated with Laubies and became a life-long devotee of visual art and artists, engaging in many collaborations. Unlike Pound, however, his choices of artistic partners ranged far and wide, including figurative as well as abstract artists, the fugitive as well as the fundamental. Creeley has written of his early days: "Possibly I hadn't as yet realised that a number of American painters had already made the shift I was myself so anxious to accomplish, that they had, in fact, already begun to move away from the insistently *pictorial*… to a manifest directly of the *energy* inherent in the materials." In New York, he gravitated to the famed Cedar Tavern, where the painters congregated. As Creeley noted: "Possibly the attraction the artists had for people like myself… has to do with that lovely, usefully uncluttered directness of perception and act we found in so many of them. I sat for hours on end listening to Franz Kline… fascinated by literally all that he had to say."

While Creeley admired the painters' directness, his poems do not reveal an obviously *visual* debt to the painters. Charles Olson did hope to open for poetry a psychological immediacy predicated on a visual impact derived from that of modern visual artists. His influential essay, *Projective Verse*, has as one of its main principles the conception of the page as a ground. Mallarmé had much earlier, in his poem *Un coup de dés jamais n'abolira le hasard*, opened up the poetic page in terms of word placement and typography; Olson added the imperative that poetic creation take place on the page, much as the Abstract Expressionists' creation took place on the canvas. He also proposed that the visual layout of a poem reflect the breathing and rests desired by the writer.

Creeley went on to maintain important ties with artists; his collaborations with around 30 of them were on view in the 1999 exhibition 'In Company: Robert Creeley's Collaborations'. Among those he worked with were Georg Baselitz, Francesco Clemente, Jim Dine, Bobbie Louise Hawkins, Alex Katz, R B Kitaj, Marisol, Susan Rothenberg and Robert Therrien. Creeley embraced the arts, particularly visual arts and music, connecting to many others he saw as trying to break from aesthetic and social restrictions he felt straitjacketed by in the 1950s, resulting in an ever-expanding world of fellow-travellers he defined as an all-important "company".

In the late 1950s to the late 1960s, Wallace Berman found his own company, much of it overlapping with Creeley's. Berman would be considered a fugitive artist, eschewing the path of gallery and museum exhibitions of his work and laying much emphasis on art as a significant factor in lived relationships. Like Creeley's, Berman's company was diverse, a shifting world of poets, artists and musicians on the West Coast of the United States, moving between Los Angeles and San Francisco. Within that world, Berman was central, attracting the likes of William Burroughs, Allen Ginsberg, Dennis Hopper, Walter Hopps, Philip Lamantia, Henry Miller, David Meltzer, Dean Stockwell and John Wieners, and lesser-known people, some of them cult figures or drifters who burned out young, others, such as Bruce Conner, Jack Smith, or Jess, eccentric talents who have carved out places in art history. Berman made his voice heard primarily through his publication *Semina* (1955–1964): sheafs of poems and images he printed himself and mailed out to a select audience (you could not subscribe or buy it anywhere). Hybridity was prized by Berman's circle. There was the feeling that an artistic statement could be made in whatever medium the artist chose – literary, visual, musical, cinematographic.

Today's interactions between poets and visual artists take place less in the amorphous space of personal relationships, as they did with the *Semina* gang, and more often within the specified confines of a book. Often, poet and artist do not even know each other before agreeing to share space between the covers. A good example of this kind of action is French publisher Gervais Jassaud, who has been making small editions of books as Collectif Génération since 1969, often working with hybrid figures. His publications begin with a text by a contemporary author, many times a poet. Jassaud then ponders an armature that can appropriately enfold the text, with a hand-made design by a visual artist. Each project has its own solutions, with specific ways of opening and folding and display of text. He will often create several versions of a book – the same words embellished by different artists. Poet and critic Barry Schwabsky, whose poem *Hidden Figure* was published by Jassaud with work by Jessica Stockholder and, separately, with art by Katharina Grosse, has noted: "Collaboration depends on a complicity

Various front covers
of *Semina* editions
1-9, edited by
Wallace Berman
(1955-1964)

Wallace Berman
Self Portrait,
Crater Lane (1955)

that goes well beyond the sympathy that a critic may have for a given artist's work." Schwabsky's complicity is far from Pound's desire to find a partner with whom to do battle against the world; it is also distinct from Creeley's and Berman's wide-ranging personae. Schwabsky, in fact, did not know Stockholder before their book project began.

The idea that one person can control the means of production and distribution brings Jassaud's projects close to the way poets think and work. After all, most poetry is published by poet-run small presses. Ruth Lingen, who has made artists' books since the 1970s, sometimes using texts by poets, works in a similar fashion. Her books make themselves felt as physical objects: written, hand-set, designed, printed and bound by Lingen. She has also worked with Stockholder on a book collaboration with a poet: *Led Almost By My Tie*, with text by Jeremy Sigler. The mesmerising variety of textures and materials on which the poem is printed is as important to the experience of the publication as the poet's words.

Jassaud and Lingen are creating venues where poets and visual artists can come face to face. These share something with Berman's *Semina*, in that by their nature they have a limited audience, yet the exclamatory force of their materials and presentation ensures their impact will be felt repeatedly for years to come. Only time will tell how significant today's reinvention of the book will be. Like John Cage and the New York School poets, today's poets take life-force from the liquids and solids of works of art. Unlike Cendrars and Pound, they do not seek the visual arts as vehicles to greater success. Rather, they find in visual artists a common desire to emulate an art form other than their own. That desire to come together is powerful because it works both ways, and here we are able to learn, in a way we could not from earlier artists, what the similarities are between poetry and the visual arts.

Vincent Katz is a poet, translator, art critic, editor and curator. He is the editor of the poetry and arts journal VANITAS *and of Libellum Books. He collaborated with Francesco Clemente on the artist's book* Alcuni Telefonini *(Granary Books, 2008).*

Polish Art: As a year-long season of exhibitions focusing on Polish art begins nationwide, TATE ETC. brings together four Polish art professionals to discuss why art from their country is not better known abroad and why it should be

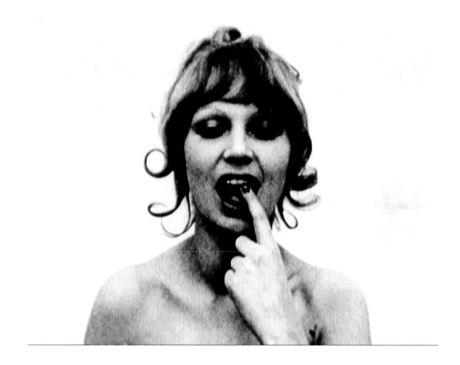

Still from **Natalia LL**'s *Consumer Art* (1974) 16mm film, silent, 15min 53sec

THE REAL EXCHANGE BETWEEN EAST & WEST

BY ANDA ROTTENBERG, MICHAL WOLINSKI, LUKASZ GORCZYCA & JAROSLAW SUCHAN

Part of **KwieKulik's** performance *Activities with the Head (3 Parts)* performed at Labitynt Gallery, Lublin, 1978

ANDA ROTTENBERG

The existence of the Iron Curtain did not allow for much exchange of information between East and West. Only certain artists managed to get out and make a name for themselves, such as Tadeusz Kantor or Magdalena Abakanowicz. The main factor keeping up the Iron Curtain was propaganda, but Poles did not believe the propaganda they were fed, while people in the West did. Until 1989 or so many critics, artists and museum directors found it inconceivable that there could be something going on in Poland under the communist regime. So they didn't look for anything. As a result of that propaganda, the view was that only the art that emerged in Poland after 1989 was interesting and important. Being art made in a country open to other countries, it was believed to be influenced by non-Polish traditions. This is still the case. We get critics, curators and museum directors coming here and asking about the post-1989 generation, and we're happy that there's a demand for their work around the world, but it's also worth thinking about the traditions that generation drew on.

MICHAL WOLINSKI

The act of looking back to the 1950s, 1960s and 1970s is something of an exotic expedition. In my magazine *Piktogram* we like to showcase the lesser-known aspects of those times, as there are many interesting phenomena that were previously ignored or misjudged. For example, KwieKulik's (Przemyslaw Kwiek and Zofia Kulik) struggle against official state-controlled art institutions for neo-avant-garde art strategies and new media. They were developing their art in a specific political and economical context of society under the communist regime, and were influenced by ideas such as cybernetics or Oskar Hansen's "Open Form" (an architecturally-driven, radical humanist utopia). They were anti-object-orientated materialists who believed – in a utopian way – that they would be able to change visual communication in the public sphere. They experimented with "visual games", collective activities and interactions. We are now getting a lot of young curators coming here who have a different attitude to Polish art. They have not been looking for the obvious artists such as Kantor or Abakanowicz, but for those such as Ewa Partum, who recently re-created her 1971 performance piece *Active Poetry* in the Turbine Hall at Tate Modern. She was shown next to Carl Andre (*Poetry Reading*), Martin Creed (*Words*) and films by Polish artists from different generations (*Image/Text*) selected by me and Lukasz Ronduda. Most of the curators we meet are well-informed and interested in Polish contemporary art, and they are curious to explore any intergenerational connections.

Ewa Partum's Warsaw performance *Active Poetry* (1971)

LUKASZ GORCZYCA — It's not true to say that there was no exchange between East and West. Especially after 1956, the exchange was vibrant. An example is the exhibition 'Fifteen Polish Painters' at the Museum of Modern Art, New York, in 1961. And in the 1970s there was a generation of Conceptual artists – Jan Swidzinski, Natalia LL and the Wroclaw art scene – who were part of the international Conceptual art circuit. I think the reason for the gap in perception from outside was the lack of any institutional partner in Poland prepared to work with international museums. Remember the story of Picasso visiting Poland in 1948 to attend the Peace Congress. He offered to donate twenty of his paintings to the National Museum in Warsaw as long as somebody from the institution would go and select works from his studio. Ultimately, the museum received a collection of ceramic plates because nobody could go.

ANDA ROTTENBERG — Well, you have to remember that the Central Committee of the Communist Party was in charge of everything, and it was obvious there could be no immediate relations between Polish institutions and foreign ones. In the case of Picasso, Stanislaw Lorentz, the National Museum's director, who was very influential, could have visited Picasso, but he didn't like his work.

JAROSLAW SUCHAN — I once did an interview with Marian Warzecha, who took part in the 'Fifteen Polish Painters' show in New York as a very young artist. He attracted a lot of interest and was invited to take part in another show at MoMA, 'Art of

Assemblage', which included work by Picasso, Jasper Johns and other important artists. As a result the legendary New York gallerist Leo Castelli reportedly asked him to join his gallery on condition that he moved to America, or would be able to travel to the US any time the need arose. Warzecha returned to Poland, but was denied a passport and lost the chance of a lifetime. There were many political and administrative restrictions that made any artistic exchange between Poland and the West very difficult. But perhaps it was also because the relationship between art in Poland and communist Europe and in the West resembled a typical one between the metropolis (or centre) and the periphery. The metropolis perceives itself as the place where real things happen and is interested in what happens in the provinces only if it proves to be something exotic. When Poland emerged from Stalinism and Social Realism during the 1950s and 1960s, it turned out that it had its own modern art – abstract painting, art *informel*, assemblage, etc – just as in the West, but as it was in a communist country, it was seen as exotic.

ANDA ROTTENBERG   I agree with your metropolitan theory and that conditions here were difficult, but those in Russia were even more difficult and yet people took suitcases full of dissident art out of Russia from 1970 onwards. I met them in 1974, and they were living very comfortably. They might not have been the best artists around, but they were in opposition to official art. They did well because people from the West were queuing up wanting to smuggle their work out of the Soviet Union, and they paid in dollars. This was not something that happened in Poland, but that's because Russia was still a great imperial power, while Poland wasn't.

JAROSLAW SUCHAN   The visual history of central Europe after 1945 is a blank slate for most of the gallery-goers, curators and critics in the West. But the situation is slowly changing. Those who initially were interested only in young Polish artists are beginning to look back to earlier periods. For example, there has recently been an exhibition entitled 'Starting From Scratch; Art & Culture in Europe and the United States 1945–1949' at the Musée des Beaux-Arts de Lyon, which included post-war paintings by Andrzej Wroblewski. He was a great figurative painter who died in 1957, but strongly influenced Polish art from the 1960s to the 1980s. The question is, however, to what extent such initiatives reflect the fascination with another exoticism and to what extent do they come from the serious will to redefine the Western view of tradition, modernism and the avant-garde?

Andrzej
Wroblewski
Rozstrzelanie V
(1949)
Oil on canvas
120×90.5cm

Andrzej
Wroblewski
Rozstrzelanie VI
(1949)
Oil on canvas
120×90cm

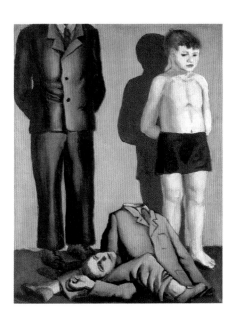 

'The Real Exchange Between East & West'

ANDA ROTTENBERG   It's still an aspect of the metropolitan viewpoint, because there is such a thing as aesthetic custom, a set of norms, a template developed in other countries that one superimposes on the art of this region in order to map it out better. I remember somebody looking at a Wroblewski painting and saying that one of the legs was done in the manner of Picasso. It's as if nothing else mattered. So until we get rid of this aesthetic habit, we will not be able to bring other values, viewpoints or traditions into the picture.

MICHAL WOLINSKI   I used the term "exotic expedition" in an ironic sense because that's how some people see it, though there is always a certain risk during such an expedition. We were talking about propaganda, censorship, ignorance and the opportunism of official institutions and official critics, not to mention the lack of commercial galleries. Add to that the fact that artists worked in a context of complex limitations – in the 1960s state policy dictated that no more than fifteen per cent of the works in a show were to be abstract, but then abstract or "pure" art began to be tolerated and even came to be seen as useful for propaganda. Sometimes it is a risky operation to revise existing judgments about artists' work and attitudes. Especially when they were trying to overstep the limitations and break out of safe frames of pure art. Or when people from other fields, such as architects, started to make art. Avant-garde architects could not carry out their projects on the scale they wanted, so they experimented with space in the galleries or in theory. This was the case with Oskar Hansen and Stanislaw Zamecznik, who developed environment art in the 1950s. Meanwhile, their partner, Lech Tomaszewski, moved into theory and began conducting remarkable research and exploring the most sophisticated branch of mathematics, namely topology. He also studied the fourth dimension, applying the imagination and intuition that making art requires to the study of topology. He made extraordinary things: projects on paper or small models that were later destroyed, things that were never before attempted in either art or topology. It was the next step, a kind of neo-avant-garde approach in the sense that he went beyond art. He wanted his work to be useful. He wanted an entirely new way of thinking about space that would inspire the imagination of artists. It was, in its way, a next step after Cubism, Futurism and Russian Constructivism.

Installation view of *Colour in Space* by Wojciech Fangor and Stanislaw Zamecznik (1959)

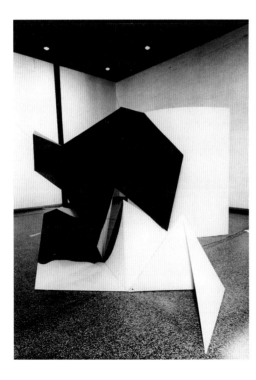

Lech Tomaszewski *Boomenrang* (1962) Chamot clay (original destroyed)

JAROSLAW SUCHAN   There's another possible reason why the interest of the West in Polish art was so intermittent. Maybe it was because those institutions in Poland that were able to promote art abroad preferred certain values and artistic phenomena that were too consistent with the Western image of what the art of a given period should be like. Perhaps they didn't sufficiently stress things that were on the sidelines from the Western perspective and from our perspective as well.

ANDA ROTTENBERG   That is a very good point.

JAROSLAW SUCHAN   The artists who took part in 'Fifteen Polish Painters', such as Wojciech Fangor and Aleksander Kobzdej, were selected, as far as I know, partly by the Americans and partly by Polish decision-makers who had a say in whose work could be shown abroad. It is typical that whenever any Polish art from outside the mainstream was shown abroad, it was not because Polish institutions promoted it, but because the world took notice on its own.

ANDA ROTTENBERG   Having followed the art scene since at least the late 1960s, I need to say that in Poland there were really two art circles that never overlapped or permeated each other. One was that of official art – which was backed by artistic institutions. There was a hierarchy with the Central Committee at the top, then the board of the Polish Artists' Union which toed the Party line, the Culture Ministry which also did what the Party required and the mainstream institutions that tried to get as much as they could across, but without overstepping the boundaries. And then, since 1964, there was the fringe: art that was the most neo-avant-garde, that shattered the moulds of art, and consciously established itself on the sidelines. The people and groups Michal mentioned – Robakowski, KwieKulik – were constantly in touch. Despite attempts to do so, the two circles didn't intermesh as there were such differences between them. Naturally, official magazines such as *Kultura* or *Polityka* wrote badly about the fringe artists when they wrote about them at all. They ridiculed people such as Ewa Partum, Andrzej Partum and KwieKulik. That style of criticism survived well into the 1990s. So this dichotomy in Polish art was perpetuated.

JAROSLAW SUCHAN   I would say the official and the less official did cross over. Also, the concept of official art supported by the state changed with time. What had been unacceptable for the communist authorities in 1958 and the early 1960s, when the quota for fifteen per cent abstraction was introduced, was different by the 1970s, when abstraction was officially sanctioned. It was seen then by First Secretary Edward Gierek as a way for Poland to be perceived internationally as a normal democracy (in the Western sense), a consumer economy with advertising and contemporary art. At that time artists such as Henryk Stazewski, Tadeusz Kantor, Magdalena Abakanowicz or Wladyslaw Hasior were exhibited in official art institutions, the books about them were edited by official publishing houses and their works were acquired by the national museums. The reason I'm saying this is that people in the West sometimes believe that Poland was like 1970s and 1980s Russia, with an official art circuit producing Socialist Realist works and an underground arty scene. But in Poland, after 1956 when Stalinism and Socialist Realism were rejected, the situation was much more complex.

ANDA ROTTENBERG   The structures or models inside Poland were only a partial obstacle to its art being understood internationally. There is another, more general, point worth mentioning. The late curator and critic Harald Szeemann said that 95 per cent of people learn about art by ear. First somebody hears a name and finds out that there is an aesthetic value attached to that name. Only then will they take an interest in that work. If someone hasn't heard a name before, they won't have the courage to admit it. That's why the name Alina Szapocznikow didn't mean anything to anyone for such a long time outside Poland. I mounted an exhibition of her work eleven years ago, and I tried to offer it around the world. Not a single person expressed any interest in her. Now, ten years on, if some of her work hadn't been shown at Documenta in Kassel, and if it hadn't finally become available on the market, directors of the great museums would still not recognise the value of her art. It's a similar case with Wróblewski, who represented a different kind of aesthetic and gave rise to a school of art in Poland that returned to the object, to observation. Today, there is a tendency to look for reminiscences of Conceptualism, there are post-Conceptual shows, there is a revival of interest in that period around the world. And that's why the artists Michal and the critic Lukasz Ronduda specialise in are attracting attention abroad. But this is not an objectively historical viewpoint. It is another case of taking advantage of a trend, or being in tune with the times.

Alina Szapocznikow
Leg (1965)
Granite and bronze
76×76×46cm

LUKASZ GORCZYCA   Yes. Apart from art histories that have a universal voice, there are also local histories and cultures.

JAROSLAW SUCHAN   The point is that certain local cultures are still seen as dominant, as being manifestations of universal culture. In the early 1990s the American critic Peter Schjeldahl wrote a piece about Miroslaw Balka in which he wondered how he managed to become an international success. He thought it was because Balka was able to translate his very particular experience as a central European artist into the idiom of international or universal art. To me that is a perfect example of metropolitan, self-centred perspective. I don't accept the concept of a universal idiom in contemporary art, or any other art for that matter. There is no such thing: every idiom was developed somewhere, in some place. And those places are usually the centres of economic and political power.

LUKASZ GORCZYCA   I believe that the universal idiom is also cracking in the Western centres that "invented" and played with the idea of modern and/or contemporary art, such as Paris, New York, London and Berlin. For example, the work of the utopian architecture group Archigram, or of, say, the outsider artist Henry Darger, is going against the grain of the universalist idiom, and is now becoming a significant part of mainstream culture.

MICHAL WOLINSKI   Yes. But when I am talking about attempts to revise achievements of architects such as Hansen and Stanislaw Zamecznik, artists such as KwieKulik and Marek Konieczny, or artist-film-makers from Workshop of The Film Form (Jozef Robakowski or Pawel Kwiek), I am also trying to highlight their importance in comparison with the current art of the younger or middle generation of artists who are successful in the West, such as Piotr Uklanski, Pawel Althamer, Artur Zmijewski and Monika Sosnowska. Their art didn't come out of nowhere. Nor could they have been infused with certain things because art history in Poland left much to be desired.

ANDA ROTTENBERG   I would say each of these artists follows another tradition. In the case of Artur Zmijewski, he represents a very specific attitude, that of a militant artist who's on the side of what we might arbitrarily call the oppressed minority, be it the disabled, or national minorities. He plumbs areas of social hypocrisy, addressing issues of the marginalisation of certain people within society. And he's closely associated with a left-wing magazine, *Krytyka Polityczna*. These subjects had never been taken up by Polish art, with the possible exception of Joanna Rajkowska. He's an outstanding artist who's become an established presence in Polish art.

LUKASZ GORCZYCA   However, it took a very long time for him to be noticed. Perhaps that was due to the fact that his earlier work, such as *Out for a Walk* (2000), where he asked paralysed people to walk, was so vulgar, savage and alien that nobody was able to stomach it. But thanks to the fact that his art took on a clear political and discursive position, and began telling stories, creating narratives about contemporary social relations, national chauvinism…

MICHAL WOLINSKI   But isn't Zmijewski saying what Western critics and curators want to hear? Isn't it politically correct to some extent?

Group portrait of (left to right)
Piotr Uklanski, Monika Szwajewska,
Marek Konieczny and Cezary
Bodzianowski (1991)

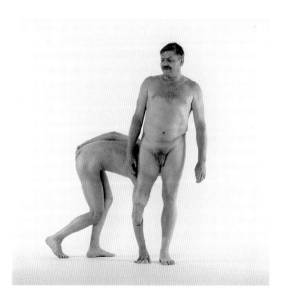

Artur Zmijewski
Eye for an Eye
(1998)
From a series
of twenty
photographs
Dimensions
variable

'The Real Exchange Between East & West'

ANDA ROTTENBERG   Definitely not… It was very politically incorrect in Poland for many years.

JAROSLAW SUCHAN   There is a point here concerning the change that occurred in Zmijewski's art: you said that he shows the phenomena related to the socially excluded from a very defined standpoint. But he assumed that standpoint some time ago, also through his institutional relationship with *Krytyka Polityczna*. His earlier works, however, are so difficult to accept precisely because they show reality stripped bare. The artist refrains from commentary, and does not help us to take the comfortable position of being on the right side. It wasn't a critique, it was an in-your-face exposing.

LUKASZ GORCZYCA   I still believe that his alliance with *Krytyka Polityczna* is yet another of his cynical artistic games. He's decided to use *Krytyka*, thinking he can use it in an equally drastic and provocative way as his work with the disabled.

JAROSLAW SUCHAN   Well, he is certainly an influential figure, though I think the distance between the generations is too slight for him to become a mentor for younger artists, or at least they would not be willing to admit to succumbing to his influence.

LUKASZ GORCZYCA   My experience with some of the artists I know or work with – Wilhelm Sasnal, Rafal Bujnowski, or the younger ones such as Janek Simon – is that they take entirely different positions artistically or politically from Zmijewski or Althamer. Whereas the latter grew up in a certain artistic tradition that can be traced back to Hansen and Grzegorz Kowalski, the people I'm speaking about make their work in a spirit of negation. They grew up unable to identify or involve themselves with a specific tradition that appeared to them as weak or compromised. We grew up in the late-communist era, which was then visibly but slowly falling apart, and started adult life in a new capitalist reality. It means our "past" was automatically considered "weak" in comparison with "new times", but we have learned to remain distanced from the new as it is probably just another artificial construction of the reality. I would just like to say that different artistic traditions were not so formative for my generation compared with "bare life" going on in a moment which was (still is?) historically extremely interesting. The tradition of 1980s painting was not a relevant benchmark. What went on in Kowalski's studio in the 1990s – the focus on a transgressive, self-expressive kind of body art, practised by Kozyra, Althamer, Zmijewski and others – was not a point of reference either, because there was a rejection of the very strong academic streak that milieu had. Theirs was a politically committed art, but only on a discursive, philosophical level. Consequently, the younger generation produced what I would call a zero syndrome, starting from scratch. Hence their art usually verges on the psychedelic or the absurd. And since public institutions have struggled to offer support, a lot of art made by young artists in the late 1990s was purely a critique of institutions. For example, Hubert Czerepok made a work where he shipped an empty crate to a gallery because the gallery had told him that it could only cover the cost of shipping. It was an attempt to establish a new order among the ruins.

ANDA ROTTENBERG   It has to be said that it's much easier to work with dead artists. That's the case with Edward Krasinski, who began to be widely known only when he was so ill that he had no influence over what was happening with his art. Wlodzimierz Borowski, who died recently, inevitably threw a spanner in the works whenever anyone wanted to help him to make a career. In this respect he was the most consistent of all Polish artists. There's a hope that, in the near future, someone will take an interest in his output and describe it,

Detail of **Jan Simon**'s interactive installation *Carpet Invaders* (2002)

Detail of **Jan Simon**'s performance *Six-Day Week* (2004)

Rafal Bujnowski
Visa Portrait
(2004)
Oil on canvas
35×35cm

because he's one of those people who are not known even in Poland, much less internationally. He said that what mattered most to him in art was artistic attitude and not what he made. (I was there when he burned several dozen of his objects). Among the "undiscovered" attitudes in Poland that greatly influenced successive generations of artists, and established a school of thinking in radical terms, his was one that has never found successors – because no one was ever as radical. But at least his work was invoked, and maybe the time has come for the world to take an interest in that attitude.

A series of Polish-related exhibitions across the country in association with *Polska!Year (which has been organised by the Adam Mickiewicz Institute) includes 'Goshka Macuga', Whitechapel Art Gallery, London, until 18 April 2010; 'Symbolism in Poland and Britain', Tate Britain, until 21 June; 'Jozef Robakowski', Ikon Gallery, Birmingham, 1 – 24 May; 'Tadeusz Kantor', Sainsbury Centre for Visual Arts, Norwich, 2 June – 30 August; 'Artur Zmijewski', A Foundation, Liverpool, and Cornerhouse, Manchester, September – December; group show curated by Paulina Olowska, Camden Art Centre, London, 18 September – 15 November; 'Robert Kusmierowski', Barbican Art Gallery, London, 25 September – 3 January. 'Miroslaw Balka and Pawel Althamer', Modern Art Oxford, January – March, is part of Polska!Year. Eight works by Edward Krasinski entered Tate Collection in 2007.*

Anda Rottenberg is a freelance art historian, critic and exhibition curator. She is former director of the Zacheta National Art Gallery, Warsaw (1993–2001) and the programme director of the Warsaw Museum of Modern Art (2006/2007). Michal Wolinski is founder and editor-in-chief of Piktogram *magazine. Lukasz Gorczyca is an art critic and founder of Raster Gallery, Warsaw. Jaroslaw Suchan is an art historian and critic and is current director of Museum Sztuki, Lodz.*

This conversation took place at the Piktogram *magazine office in Warsaw. Translated from the Polish by Artur Zapalowski.*

Edward
Krasinski
laying out
*Intervention
4, Zig Zag* in
his studio
(1970)

© Paulina Krasinska. Courtesy Generali Foundation

Edward Krasinski
alongside his
sculpture *Pulawy
3* (1968),
photographed
by Eustachy
Kossakowski

Installation view
of **Edward
Krasinski**'s *Room
no.10, Atelier
Puzzle* in the
Foksal Gallery
(1994)

'The Real Exchange Between East & West'

John William Inchbold
Detail of *Suggestive Study*, *Paradise (Head of a Girl and a Bird of Paradise)* (1864-1865)
Pencil and watercolour on paper 25.5 × 17.8 cm

Photograph: Tate

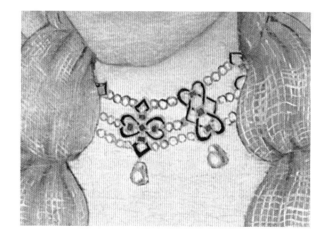

Seventeenth-century British School
Details of *The Cholmondeley Ladies* (c.1600-1610)
Oil on wood 107.4 × 191.4 cm

Photograph: Tate

Steve Jones on John William Inchbold's *Suggestive Study, Paradise (Head of a Girl and a Bird of Paradise)* (1864–1865)

As a geneticist, my job is to make sex boring. Artists attempt the opposite: to add romance to the prosaic rules of biology. Darwin wrote: "The sight of a feather in a peacock's tail, whenever I gaze at it, makes me feel sick." Why did only males have one and why was it so clumsy? How could natural selection – inherited differences in the ability to reproduce – do that? Selection, he saw, was a two-part exam. The first paper, survival, was simple, but the second – reproduction – was more subtle.

Any attribute of one gender favoured by the other ("beauty", as we call it) would become common, however absurd it appeared and however much, within limits, it reduced the chances of staying alive. Sexual selection explained many of the joys of nature – flowers, birdsong and baboons' bottoms included. Darwin also claimed: "Of all the causes which have led to the differences in external appearance between the races of man… sexual selection has been by far the most important."

Inchbold's painting is in that tradition: the blonde as the human Bird of Paradise; the highest and most beauteous form of all. Unfortunately, Darwin was wrong. Blondes emerged only 5,000 years ago when farming spread to north-west Europe. The combination of lousy weather and a dismal diet led to a shortage of vitamin D, and to rickets. Those with the lightest skins (and hair) were favoured because sunlight could get in and make the missing substance: hence the flaxen-haired subject. *Head of a Girl and a Plate of Muesli* would not, perhaps, have the same impact.

Steve Jones is professor of genetics and head of the research department of genetics, evolution and environment, University College London.
— Suggestive Study, Paradise (Head of a Girl and a Bird of Paradise) *was purchased as part of the Oppé Collection with assistance from the National Lottery through the Heritage Lottery Fund in 1996 and is included in 'Endless Forms; Charles Darwin, Natural Science and the Visual Arts' at the Fitzwilliam Museum, Cambridge, 16 June – 4 October.*

William Fiennes on *The Cholmondeley Ladies* (British School, c.1600–1610)

My ruff was a sort of amphitheatre of lace and bone that screened off large sectors of the world: I could only see what lay ahead, as if I were a language with no past or present tenses. The artist (I never learned his name) kept stepping away, frowning as he looked from me and my sister to his version of us on the wide board and back again, as if confused by the quantity of women in the room, our original doubling now redoubled in his painting. All this time my boy was quiet and still, even as I wished for him to shout or scream and so be the disruption of which I was myself no longer capable. I thought about the little gasp he'd given that morning when he saw our church's spire narrowing above him into the blue, and of how, when they used both hands to pull the cords

of my corset tighter, my maids were like mariners rigging a ship, hoisting the sails: it helped to think of some part of myself unfurling even as the servants hemmed me in. I'd noticed, as they arranged us against the pillows, her necklace, intricate with pendants, and been grateful for my simple carcanet of garnets and pearls. I felt the weight of my child in my hands and the cool lightness of metals and stones on my bare skin. I heard my sister breathing. We would wait a long time for men to give the word and release us to our separate chambers.

William Fiennes is a writer based in London. His most recent book, The Music Room, *is published by Picador.*
— The Cholmondeley Ladies *was presented anonymously in 1955 and is on display at Tate Britain.*

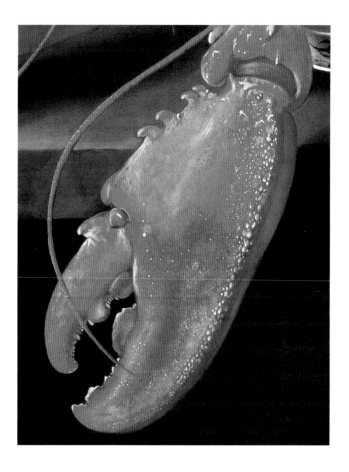

Charles
Collins
Detail of
*Lobster on a
Delft Dish*
(1738)
Oil on canvas
70.5×91cm

Daria Martin
Still from *In
the Palace*
(2000)
16mm film,
colour and
audio track,
7min

Valentine Warner on
Charles Collins's *Lobster on a Delft Dish* (1738)

I love lobsters. They are worriers and I empathise with their grumpy but harmless nature. However, they are delicious to eat…

Lobster Mojo de Ajo (serves 2–4)
1 x 900g live lobster
For the mojo de ajo sauce
1 generous head garlic
roughly 100ml light olive oil
2 plump chipotle chillies, finely chopped
1 large lime, freshly squeezed
½ tsp flaked sea salt
fresh coriander leaves, to garnish
lime wedges, to serve

First peel all the garlic cloves and chop to medium fine. Put in a small pan and cover with sunflower oil. Bring the oil up to a gentlest simmer and set the heat, allowing the little lemonade lines of tiny bubbles to fizz from the garlic. Do not overheat or boil at any cost or the garlic will burn. Scientific attention is needed. The garlic is ready when it begins to turn an old ivory colour. This will take ten to fifteen minutes. At this point drop in the finely chopped chipotles, the squeezed lime juice and the

salt. Thirty seconds after adding these turn off the heat and allow the mixture to stand for at least three hours.

To cook the lobster, light the barbecue and leave to burn until a light dusting of grey ash covers the coals. (You can also cook the lobster under the grill for four minutes on each side.) Do not remove the bands from the lobster's claws until you have killed it, as this will only result in severed fingers on the kitchen floor. When killing your dinner do it swiftly, as squeamish scrapings on the shell with a knife will only distress the lobster. Lay the lobster flat on a board and hold it down firmly with a cloth to prevent it arching up. Picking up a large heavy knife, deftly and without hesitation drive the point into the middle of its head and on to the board. Lever the blade down to cut between the eyes. Turn it round. Put the blade back into where you made the first entry and cut the other way straight down and through the middle of the tail section. Remove the green parts inside the lobster's head and throw away with the snipped off elastic bands. Taking a rolling pin, crack the claws without pulverising them and leaving

the shell on. Brush the tail meat generously with the garlic oil, but not the tasty sediment in the bottom. Salt lightly. Put the lobster on the barbecue, flesh side down. Cook for four minutes before turning on to the shell side and cooking until it has all turned vibrant red (approximately another four minutes). Lift off the rack, and put on a serving plate. Spoon over the sauce liberally, ensuring you get lots of garlic and chilli from the bottom and less oil. Garnish the empty head cavity with coriander and lime wedges for squeezing. Serve with cold beer.

Valentine Warner trained as a painter before becoming a chef. His second BBC TV series, What To Eat Now – More Please, *is broadcast this summer.*
— Lobster on a Delft Dish *was purchased in 1988.*

Carol Bove on
Daria Martin's *In the Palace* (2000)

I first met Daria shortly after I had seen and fallen in love with her film *Birds*. I had been at the New York opening of her first exhibition there. Despite a well-attended evening, when I spotted her she was leaning against the wall on her own. I was too shy and insecure to compliment her on the piece, which seems crazy now.

When we met a few years later in London we spoke briefly about growing up in the San Francisco Bay area. We must have been talking about the human potential of movements, or cults, or whatever other forces guided the energies of California-seekers in those days. This led to her description of a dance class she had recently attended called "Body Weather". I wish I could steal that name. Body weather. It

expresses a condensation of everything that dance is and what the body could mean in performance art. Both New Age and also drab and materialist; Gaia, the mother goddess and body of the earth, plus pure pragmatism. The integration of one's self with the environment and receptivity to changing forces. A spiritual practice that seeks to develop an accurate picture of the present physical moment. Experience. A figure in a landscape.

What could they possibly have done in such a class? I think she had been disappointed by it. I can't remember. As I recall, and my memory of her description is vague, the participants were instructed to stand face to face with the other people and talk about the body and about the weather.

The instructor demonstrated the action using the mannerisms and affectations of Brecht-style performance, but softened and modified by a hard-core meditator's sensibility. And? I think the conversation took us someplace else, or stopped abruptly at that point.

We only ever met once or twice more in passing or at an opening, but I have a special affection for her work since I've been a witness from the beginning. And I always think about it through the lens of "Body Weather".

Carol Bove is an artist who lives and works in New York. Her exhibition at Tate St Ives runs from 16 May to 20 September.
— In the Palace *was purchased in 2000.*

'MicroTate'

BUSINESS OR PLEASURE?

In a seaside town, pleasure, or at least its less blatantly sensual cousin, leisure, is the business. If asked to imagine a picture of an English seaside scene, I suspect that few of us would put two large men in heavy-looking dark suits in the frame. Or, for that matter, slap bang in the middle of a promenade. And yet here they are in this photograph – an image loosed from a magazine, perhaps for its very incongruity, by Francis Bacon and now in the Tate archive.

Yellowing and on paper so scratched it appeared cat-clawed rather than dog-eared, this clipping was tucked inside a file labelled "Portraits, political". It was lurking below a photo of Stalin daubed in red paint. Disconcertingly, that pigmentation concentrated, accidentally or otherwise, around the Soviet leader's eyes, aroused thoughts of David Bowie circa *Aladdin Sane*. Apart from a faint green smear, the suit men had been spared such ornamentation. Possibly Bacon felt them surreal enough not to bother – there is a whiff of Magritte's *La Reproduction Interdite* (c.1937)about the backs of those heads after all. Though, I'll admit, the effect is somewhat undermined by the pudginess of those necks.

Since there is no supporting information and their faces can't be seen, who they are or what business they have here – both at the beach and among Bacon's papers – remains pleasingly indeterminate. That uncertainty is a distinct boon to anyone, like myself, who finds entertaining wayward, or patently absurd, speculations a good way to pass an hour or so. And, surely, if we look at an artist's ephemera,

it is to speculate – did doodle X lead to masterpiece Y?

With Bacon, a consummate scavenger, a man for whom a single still from Eisenstein's *Battleship Potemkin* served as faithfully as the Vim and boot polish he put to work on his teeth and hair, the ratpickings hold a particular, maybe even slightly prurient, fascination. I remembered that John Deakin, bibulous snapper-in-residence to Bacon's Colony Room court, had died after a bender in Brighton. Did this seafront tableau summon up any memories of Deakin for Bacon? Or did he have ghosts of an altogether different kind in mind?

Looking at the sheer hulking mass of the figures, the breadth of shoulders, the volume of cloth seemingly deployed on the trousers, that odd concertina-like bunching at the knee, they give off a certain physical and… well, frankly, Baconesque menace. They are meaty in every sense of the word. At first glance I thought they were overdressed. But taking in the old codger in the deckchair on the left, kitted out in the droopy flat cap and long winter overcoat, I started to wonder if the reverse could be true. The idea that they might have forgone warmer clobber now made them seem all the more sinister to me.

Suddenly they'd become Goldberg and McCann, the seaside guest house henchmen from Harold Pinter's *The Birthday Party*. Or Ronnie and Reggie Kray down for the day. Off season. In a hurry. With people to see. But, no, that briefcase didn't quite fit. Bow-shaped with a brassy clasp, it was a carrier better suited to manila files

than sawn-off shotguns. This was a bag for the bureaucrat. The kind of bag the snug-bar-hogging bigwigs of Piltdown in Tony Hancock's *The Punch and Judy Man* might use. A bag where a you-scratch-my-back-I'll-scratch-yours building contract for a new marina could easily be stowed. Business for pleasure, you see. The usual distinctions, Bacon's little scrapbook offering had conspired to remind me again, tend to go adrift whenever you are by the sea.

To find out more about the Tate archive: www.tate.org.uk/research/researchservices.

Travis Elborough is the author of The Bus We Loved *and* The Long-player Goodbye. *He is currently writing a book about the English seaside.*

Magazine cutting of unidentified men from **Francis Bacon** archive

Tate archive

Subscribe Now To

Tate *Etc!*

One-year subscription:
- ☐ United Kingdom £15
- ☐ Europe £17
- ☐ Rest of World £20

for 3 issues + 1 gratis

Two-year subscription:
- ☐ United Kingdom £30
- ☐ Europe £34
- ☐ Rest of World £40

for 6 issues + 2 gratis

I enclose cheque for £ .... made payable to TATE ETC.
(Cheques accepted in pound sterling only)

Please debit my —
- ☐ Mastercard ☐ Visa ☐ Switch *(UK only)*

Cardholder's name
....

Card no
....

Expiry date   *Issue no*
....

Signature
....

Delivery address —
If this is a gift subscription, please give details of the recipient

☐ For myself   ☐ A gift

Name
....

Address
....

....

....

Zip/ Post code   *Country*
....

Email
....

Tel
....

Simply complete the form and fax to +44 (0) 20 7887 3940, or send to: TATE ETC. Subscriptions, Tate Britain, Millbank, London SW1P 4RG

... or subscribe online at www.tate.org.uk/tateetc

Last remaining copies left — Order now!

To order back issues, call +44 (0)20 7887 8959 or email *subscriptions@tate.org.uk*

TATE ETC. Subscriptions
Tate
Millbank
London SW1P 4RG

...or subscribe online at *www.tate.org.uk/tateetc*

ETC–16

Last remaining copies left — Order now!

To order back issues, call +44 (0)20 7887 8959 or email *subscriptions@tate.org.uk*